AFRICAN HISTORICAL DICTIONARIES
Edited by Jon Woronoff

Historical Dictionary

of

THE SUDAN

by

John Obert Voll

African Historical Dictionaries, No. 17

The Scarecrow Press, Inc.
Metuchen, N.J. & London
1978

Library of Congress Cataloging in Publication Data

Voll, John Obert, 1936-
    Historical dictionary of the Sudan.

        (African historical dictionaries ; no. 17)
        Bibliography: p.
        I.   Sudan--History--Dictionaries.   2.   Sudan--
History--Bibliography.   3.   Sudan--Bibliography.
I.   Title.   II.   Series.
DT. 155. 3. V64   962. 4'003   77-28798
ISBN 0-8108-1115-4

To Sudanese-American friendship.

I hope that in some small way
this work can begin to repay
my great debt to the people of the Sudan
for their hospitality and generosity

CONTENTS

EDITOR'S FOREWORD

Jon Woronoff

The Sudan, far from the best known country in Africa, is nonetheless the continent's largest country. It is also Black Africa, Muslim and Christian or animist populations, and moderate and radical regimes. Yet, this function of meeting place or crossroads is an age-old one, as is shown by its role in ancient Egypt and the more recent Anglo-Egyptian Sudan.

This wealth of history and this variety of social, religious and ethnic groups are clearly traced in the present dictionary on the Sudan. The density of its history becomes particularly great at times when the "meeting place" was a barrier, a confrontation, an invasion or a civil war. Thus a series of major events is presented leading up to the most recent conflict between north and south, so well hidden from the public that it became modern Africa's oldest and one of its bloodiest wars before many even realized that it was taking place. But the men who fought that war, and those--often the same--who concluded the peace are not forgotten. Nor are those who were prominent in a continuous series of challenges to the regime of the day.

This dictionary should certainly be enough to whet the appetite of the student first encountering the Sudan. It will also help the more initiated in the retrieval of information and facts. The contents are broad enough to cover the earliest and most recent periods, made more readily comprehensible by the chronology and the lists of rulers comprising the appendices. But the major aid is a bibliography that takes up nearly half the book, and can put the readers, and the librarian, on the path to further sources and knowledge.

Dr. John Voll's acquaintance with the Sudan is a long and a deep one, beginning with over a year's stay there in 1963-64 and later visits both to the country and to sources

vii

of research material on British policy in the Sudan, in England. And his interest extends beyond the Sudan to the broader Arab and Islamic context that is increasingly shaping it. His doctoral thesis, papers presented to various academic meetings, and a continuous stream of articles and studies on the Sudan and the Islamic world have all paved the way to this dictionary.

Jon Woronoff
Series Editor

A NOTE ON SPELLING

There are always spelling problems when a person deals with languages with two different alphabets. No single solution to the problem of writing Arabic names in the Roman alphabet has been devised. In this book an attempt has been made to find an intelligible middle ground between highly precise but uncommon academic transliteration systems and common local and journalistic spellings. As a matter of principle spelling has followed the usage in two recent and widely-used reference works on the Sudan: Area Handbook for the Democratic Republic of Sudan published by the U.S. Government Printing Office and Politics in the Sudan by Peter K. Bechtold. In this way some basic uniformity may be available to the non-specialist, English-speaking student.

In this framework it is useful to call the reader's attention to a few potential problem areas. In personal names many Sudanese have developed their own English spelling for their names. Where these spellings are well-known, as in the case of Mamoun Beheiry, Beshir Mohammed Said, or the al-Tom family, they have been used. In other cases, where a variety of spellings are used, the usage of the Area Handbook is followed. This is the case with the name of President Numayri, where other spellings--Nimeiri, Nimeri, Nimeiry--are also common. In place names, the best-known English spelling is used (Omdurman rather than Umm Durman, for example). A more careful following of academic transliteration is used in more technical terms, e.g., shaykh rather than sheik, and also for names in the earlier historical periods.

ABBREVIATIONS AND ACRONYMS

ACNS	Advisory Council for the Northern Sudan
AFESD	Arab Fund for Economic and Social Development
ALF	Azania Liberation Front
ARG	Anyidi Revolutionary Government
CPS	Communist Party of the Sudan
DUP	Democratic Unionist Party
NUP	National Unionist Party
PDP	People's Democratic Party
SACDNU	Sudan African Closed Districts National Union (see SANU)
SALF	Sudan African Liberation Front
SANU	Sudan African National Union
SCP	Communist Party of the Sudan
SSLM	South Sudan Liberation Movement
SSPG	South Sudan Provisional Government
SSU	Sudan Socialist Union
SWTUF	Sudan Workers Trade Union Federation

CHRONOLOGY OF IMPORTANT EVENTS

Pre-4000 B.C.	Paleolithic Era in the Sudan [note: dates B.C. are approximate]
4000-3500 B.C.	Mesolithic Era--Nubian and early Khartoum sites.
3500-3000 B.C.	Early Neolithic, as in Bahan Culture and Shaheinab sites.
3000-2600 B.C.	A-Group Culture in Nubia, and the beginnings of states like Yam, Setu, and Irtet.
2700-2100 B.C.	Period of growing contact with Egypt, and some Egyptian conquest in Nubia. B-Group period in Nubia.
2100-1900 B.C.	Rise of C-Group culture and relative decline of Egyptian influence in the Sudan during Egypt's First Intermediate Period.
1900-1575 B.C.	Rise of Kerma Culture and Nubian independence during Egypt's Middle Kingdom and Second Intermediate Period.
1575-1090 B.C.	Egyptian conquest and rule in the northern Sudan under the New Kingdom Pharaohs.
1090-750 B.C.	Emergence of the kingdom of Kush centered in Napata.
750-656 B.C.	Kushite conquest of Egypt and the establishment of the XXVth Dynasty.
656-590 B.C.	Kushite withdrawal back to the Sudan, with the continued survival of the Amon cult and the Kingdom of Kush at Napata.

590 B. C.   Psammetichos II invaded Nubia, sacked Napata, and probably caused the transfer of Kush's capital to Meroe.

590 B. C. - Rise and gradual decline of the Kingdom of Kush
A. D. 350   at Meroe. Strong iron age society emerged with a distinctive Sudanese culture

A. D. 350- X-Group or Ballana Culture period in Nubia--
550   the era of the Blemmyes and the development of the kingdoms of Nobatia, Alwa, and Makuria.

543-570   Conversion of rulers of the Sudanese kingdoms to Christianity.

640   Arab Muslim conquest of Egypt and beginning of Muslim contacts with the northern Sudan.

ca. 1200   Rise of the Daju dynasty in Darfur.

1300-1350   Defeat of the last Christian king in Nubia and the first Muslim king came to the throne in Dongola.

1400's   Probable time of the replacement of the Daju by the Tunjur Dynasty in Darfur.

1504   Traditional date for the fall of Soba, capital of Alwa, and the end of the last Christian state in the Sudan. Also marks the beginning of the Funj Sultanate.

1580-1660   Time of the beginning of Keira rule in Darfur.

1761   Muhammad Abu Likaylik took control of the Funj Sultanate, beginning the period of the Hamaj dominance over puppet sultans.

1820-1822   Forces from Egypt conquered much of the northern Sudan, bringing an end to the Funj Sultanate and establishing the Turco-Egyptian regime in the Sudan.

1863-1879   Introduction of anti-slavery measures by the Egyptian government.

1871-1874   Zubayr Pasha conquered Bahr al-Ghazal and Darfur.

1881   Muhammad Ahmad al-Mahdi proclaimed his mis-
            sion of Islamic reform and the Mahdist conquest
            of the Sudan began.

1885   Khartoum conquered by Mahdist forces, bringing
            an end to the Egyptian regime. In June, Mu-
            hammad Ahmad died and was succeeded by Ab-
            dallah al-Tai'ishi.

1889   Mahdist invasion of Egypt stopped at the battle
            of Toshki.

1896   Conquest began of the Mahdist state by Anglo-
            Egyptian forces.

1898   Battle of Omdurman, marking the major defeat
            of the Mahdist forces and bringing an end to the
            independent Mahdist state. British and French
            forces almost fought at Fashoda in the imperi-
            alist rivalry for control of the upper Nile valley.

1899   Anglo-Egyptian agreement defined the joint Anglo-
            Egyptian Condominium for the Sudan, legally in
            effect until Sudanese independence.

1906   Work begun on building Port Sudan, which came
            to replace Suakin as the major Sudanese harbor
            on the Red Sea.

1916   Sultan Ali Dinar in Darfur defeated, bringing an
            end to the Keira dynasty and resulting in the
            full incorporation of the province into the Anglo-
            Egyptian Sudan.

1924   Major nationalist outbreaks in the Sudan. White
            Flag League and other groups led anti-imperi-
            alist demonstrations. British reaction intensified
            by the murder of the governor-general of the Su-
            dan, Lee Stack, in Cairo. Egyptian influence
            reduced in the Sudan, military units which had
            mutinied were defeated, and nationalism sup-
            pressed.

1925   Completion of the Sennar Dam and the opening
            of the Gezira Scheme.

1931   Student strike at Gordon College over pay cuts
            for Sudanese employed by the government.

1936   Anglo-Egyptian Treaty signed, reducing the re-
            strictions on Egyptians in the Sudan.

1938   Formation of the Graduates Congress

1942   Presentation of the Graduates Congress memo-
            randum speaking in the name of the Sudanese
            and the British rejection of the claims of the
            Congress.

1943-1945   Formation of the first political parties in the
            Sudan: the Ashigga, the Umma Party, and oth-
            ers.

1944   Creation of the Advisory Council for the North-
            ern Sudan

1947   Juba Conference, where southern leaders ac-
            cepted the idea of the unification of the southern
            and northern parts of the Sudan.

1948   Opening of the Legislative Assembly.

1952   Enactment of the Self-Government Statute, which
            provided for Sudanese self-government after an
            indefinite period.

1953   Anglo-Egyptian Agreement outlining the end of
            the Anglo-Egyptian Government and initiating
            steps to self-rule. The first parliament was
            elected with a majority of seats won by the Na-
            tional Unionist Party.

1954-1955   Sudanization of the army and the administration
            with a cabinet led by Ismail al-Azhari.

1955   Equatoria Corps mutiny in the south, with many
            northerners and southerners killed, a result of
            southern fears of northern dominance.

1956   Sudanese independence proclaimed. In a polit-
            ical shift resulting from the creation of the Peo-
            ple's Democratic Party, a PDP-Umma coalition
            government led by Abdallah Khalil replaced the
            government of Ismail al-Azhari.

1958   New parliamentary elections held; the PDP-

Umma coalition continued until November, when a military government led by Ibrahim Abboud took over after a coup.

1959   Nile waters agreement with Egypt outlining Egyptian compensation for lands to be flooded by waters rising behind the Aswan Dam.

1961-1962   New constitutional law promulgated creating provincial councils and a central, national council.

1962-1963   Intensification of the conflict in the south, accompanied by the establishment of the Anya Nya and SANU.

1964   October Revolution, ousting the Abboud regime after a long series of demonstrations and strikes. A transition government was formed under the premiership of Sirr al-Khatim al-Khalifah.

1965   New elections for parliament held. A NUP-Umma Party alliance resulted in a government headed by Muhammad Ahmad Mahjub. Khartoum Round Table Conference held in an attempt to find a solution to the conflict in the southern Sudan.

1966   Split within the Umma Party, bringing down the Mahjub government, which was replaced by a cabinet led by Sadiq al-Mahdi.

1967   Muhammad Ahmad Mahjub again prime minister. The Sudan sent forces to fight in the "Six-Day" Arab-Israeli War and was host to the Arab summit conference at the end of the summer.

1968   General election held and the Mahjub government, with some changes, continued. William Deng, an important southern politician, assassinated.

1969   May Revolution, led by Ja'far al-Numayri, took control of the government. A new government established with Babikr Awadallah as prime minister and Ja'far Numayri as head of the Revolutionary Council. Among its early actions, the revolutionary government announced new policies

for the south, including amnesty and regional autonomy, and initiated a broad socialist program for economic and social development.

1970   March: Revolt led by the Ansar Imam, al-Hadi al-Mahdi, defeated. May: Banks and a number of businesses nationalized and a five-year development plan initiated. November: Sudan reached agreement with Egypt and Libya on the basic steps to be taken for an eventual tripartite federation.

1971   May: First steps leading to the creation of the Sudan Socialist Union and the new constitutional regime. July: Government taken over for a few days by a group of dissident officers. In the aftermath of the abortive coup, Communist Party leaders and others were jailed or executed. September: Popular referendum confirmed Ja'far Numayri as president.

1972   January: Sudan Socialist Union officially established, with the first SSU Congress giving its approval to the National Charter. Basic outline of the permanent constitution approved, and the SSU Political Bureau formed. March: Agreement reached between the government and southern leaders for a settlement of the conflict in the south, recognizing regional autonomy. September: Elections held for the new People's Assembly.

1973   March: Palestinians captured, then killed U.S. diplomats. Summer: Discontent over economic conditions and a state of emergency declared briefly. December: First Popular Regional Assembly for the southern region created.

1974   April: Egypt and the Sudan announced measures for closer cooperation. May: Numayri charged Libyan government with attempting to overthrow the Sudanese government. Later in year: many agreements with other Arab countries announced to help finance Sudanese agricultural and industrial development.

1975   March: Incident took place at Akobo in the south

where some soldiers were involved in southern
unrest, but basic lines of the southern settlement continued in effect. May: Major development budget announced. June and July: Further
measures of Egyptian-Sudanese cooperation announced.

1976   January: $700-million plan for agricultural de-
velopment announced, to be financed with the
help of AFESD and to involve more than 60 projects in the next decade. June: Numayri visited
United States for talks dealing with economic and
political cooperation. July: an attempted coup
for which Sadiq al-Mahdi and Libya were blamed.
August: Numayri formed a new cabinet, re-
linquishing the post of premier to Rashid al-
Tahir. October: Continuing Sudanese-Saudi
Arabian cooperation affirmed during a state visit
to the Sudan by King Khalid of Saudi Arabia.

1977   January: Continuing crisis over territorial in-
cursions with Ethiopia reached a new peak of
intensity. Numayri announced his support for
Eritrean independence. February: A major
cabinet reorganization with Rashid al-Tahir remaining prime minister. National Congress of
the Sudan Socialist Union was held and Numayri
was reelected president of the SSU, in antici-
pation of a later national referendum and presidential elections.

THE SUDAN

INTRODUCTION

The Republic of the Sudan is the largest country in
Africa. Nearly one million square miles in area, it stretches
from sandy deserts in the north to tropical rain forests in
the south. It contains a variety of peoples with differing
origins, religions, languages, and life styles. This diversity
reflects the Sudan's location in northeast Africa, linking and
combining different cultural and geographic regions.

The Sudan is both Middle Eastern and African.
Enough Sudanese are Arabs or Arabic-speaking to put the
country firmly within the Arab world, and yet, non-Arabs
are the majority of the population. Many of its major ethnic groups spread beyond the boundaries of the state. The
Sudan straddles a number of significant cultural frontiers as
well as ethnic ones: it is on the frontier between Muslim
and Christian Africa, between Nile valley civilizations and
African Sudanic cultures, between Arabic-speaking and English-speaking Africa and, at the same time, between English-
speaking and Francophone Africa. It is a transitional zone
between the cultural units of West Africa and East Africa,
and is a bridge between the Arabian Peninsula and Africa.
Many scholars suggest that the Sudan may have had an important historical role as a channel for ideas and technologies passing from the ancient Near East into Africa. Bridg-
ing a number of frontiers and including a diversity of elements, Sudanese society has emerged with profound links to
other societies and yet has created its own distinctive identity.

GEOGRAPHY

The name, "the Sudan," comes from the Arabic expression bilād al-Sūdān, meaning "the land of the blacks."
In medieval Muslim literature it was applied generally to
Africa south of the Sahara. The term, "the Sudan," has
gained a more restricted meaning in modern times, referring

1

to the broad belt of plains and savanna land stretching from the Atlantic to the Red Sea and lying between the Sahara and the forest areas. In English and Arabic the term is also used in a still more restricted sense to mean the territories south of Egypt which formed the Anglo-Egyptian Sudan (1899-1955) and the contemporary Republic of the Sudan. It was first used in this sense during the 19th century and applied to the African territories ruled by Muhammad Ali, the Ottoman governor of Egypt, and his successors.

The Republic of the Sudan has an area of 967,500 square miles or about 2.4 million square kilometers. It measures almost 1,300 miles from north to south and 1,100 from east to west. It shares borders with Egypt, Libya, Chad, the Central African Empire, Zaïre, Uganda, Kenya, and Ethiopia, and has a coastal frontier on the Red Sea. Its boundaries were largely drawn by the imperial powers, with only minor adjustments being made since independence in 1956.

The Sudan is a country of tremendous geographical diversity. The climate includes the deserts of the north, where rainfall is rare, a semi-arid belt in the central plains, and increasing rainfall further to the south. Up to 60 inches a year are received along the southern border. Vegetation tends to match this, with sparse desert growth in the north and, moving south, belts of acacia scrub and short grasses, then woodland savanna, and finally, swamps, floodlands, and rain-forest areas. Occasional mountain or high hill areas, especially Jabal Marrah, the Red Sea Hills, and the Ethiopian border highlands, interrupt these belts and have distinctive mountain vegetation.

The Nile and its tributaries are the most dominant single feature of the physical landscape. The river system cuts across the climatic and vegetation belts, providing water for irrigation, a major means of transportation, and the focus for most of the settled agricultural life and economy of the country. The Nile itself is formed by two great rivers, the Blue and White Niles, which join together at Khartoum. The White Nile enters from Uganda and crosses a large flat plain, forming the great swamp or sudd region of the south, before it reaches Khartoum. The Blue Nile rises in the Ethiopian highlands and contributes most of the floodwaters, since the White Nile loses much by evaporation in the sudd. The only major tributary north of Khartoum is the Atbara River.

Different regions of the Sudan can be identified in a variety of ways. In geological terms, one can see the dominant topological features as (1) the Nile drainage system, (2) the great eroded region of the Red Sea mountains, (3) vast plains with occasional sharp hills, (4) volcanic uplands in Darfur, and (5) southern and southeastern highlands.

Geographers have combined geological with other features and have defined as many as 12 basic regions (with many subregions), thus reflecting the great diversity of the country. A classification should include the Nile Valley in the north and central parts, where most people farm with the aid of irrigation; the western Sudan as an area of mixed nomadism and peasant agriculture; the eastern Sudan as primarily an area of nomadism but with some irrigated agricultural areas; and the southern region with a wide variety of pastoral and complex tribal agricultural societies.

Within the Sudan, certain areas have been defined by historical experience as much as geographical features. The Nile valley in the northern Sudan and southern Egypt, approximately from Aswan in Egypt to Dongola, is Nubia, a region whose peoples have maintained a cultural distinctiveness since ancient times. South of Nubia was the central area of the kingdom of Kush around the city of Meroe. It was founded on three sides by the Nile and Atbara rivers and was known as the "Island of Meroe." Further up the river valley, the area between the Blue and White Niles came to be called "the island" or the "Gezira." Finally, the southern third of the country has in the 20th century come to be spoken of as a separate region, "The South." This area was the three former provinces of Equatoria, Bahr al-Ghazal, and Upper Nile.

PEOPLE

The population of the Sudan according to provisional results of the 1973 census is 14,872,000. Many people believe that this figure is too low and some estimates of the population in the mid-70's are as high as 20 or 22 million.

Ethnic and Tribal Groupings. The inhabitants are of varying ethnic origin. The 1955/56 census listed 56 separate ethnic or major tribal groupings and 597 significant subgroupings. The Arabs make up the largest single group. Definition of this category is complex since "Arab" can refer

to ethnic, linguistic, and cultural characteristics in a variety of combinations. Some Arabs migrated to the Sudan before Islam, but the major movement was in medieval times and later. Arab nomadic tribes and traveling merchants came to the Sudan, intermarried, and settled. Thus, Arabs in the Sudan are descendants of migrating tribes, products of intermarriage, or local groups which over the centuries have become culturally Arabized. In the 1955/56 census, 39 per cent of the Sudanese identified themselves as members of Arab tribes.

Concentrated in the northern provinces, most of the Arab tribes are indentified on the basis of traditional genealogies with either the Juhayna or Jaaliyyin-Danaqla groupings of tribes. The Jaaliyyin division includes Arabized Nubians and comprises most of the settled tribes of the Nile valley and Kordofan. The Juhayna tribes appear to have come more quickly to the Sudan and more of them have retained the nomadic way of life. Included in this grouping are the great camel-herding tribes of the Kababish and Shukriyyah, and the cattle-owning Baqqara of the western provinces. Although most Sudanese Arab tribes belong to these two groups, a few, like the Kawahla and Rasha'ida, claim different ancestry.

There are also a number of non-Arab groups in the northern Sudan. The Beja tribes are possibly of ancient origin and, although Muslim now, have maintained a special cultural identity. They make up about 6 per cent of the total population and are concentrated in the eastern and Red Sea provinces. Nubians in the northern province have even earlier historical origins; some groups have maintained traditional languages while others have become quite Arabized. The 1955/56 census identified about 3 per cent of the population as Nubian. Another group, possibly related to the Nubians, is the Nuba, or inhabitants of the Nuba Mountains of southern Kordofan. This group of isolated cultivators is physically and culturally distinctive and make up almost 6 per cent of the Sudanese population. In addition to these groups there are many distinctive smaller ones, like the Fur and Zaghawa of Darfur and mixed groups in Darfunj. The largest non-Arab group in the north is made up of those peoples who have migrated relatively recently from West Africa, representing at least 13 per cent of the total population.

The tribal composition of the southern Sudan is also complex. Even the definition of major groupings has been

the subject of dispute. Perhaps the simplest is the division
into the Nilotic tribes and the Sudanic. The largest and best
known of the Nilotics are the Dinka (more than 12 per cent
of the total population), Nuer, Shilluk, and Anuak. Some
tribes, like the Bari, are called Nilo-Hamitic rather than
Nilotic by scholars using a different linguistic classification.
The largest of the Sudanic groups is the Azande in the south-
west.

Language. Linguistic diversity is closely related to
the ethnic and tribal patterns of Sudanese society. Arabic
is the official language and more than half of the population
reported Arabic as their native tongue in the 1955/56 census.
That census, however, indicated that 115 different languages,
including 26 major ones, are spoken in the Sudan. In the
north the major ones other than Arabic are the various Beja,
Nubian, Nuban, Darfurian, West African, and Funj languages.
In the south, Arabic is not as common, although its use is
increasing. English is a common alternative among educated
southerners. The major local languages are tribal, with
Dinka, Nuer, and Zande being the most widely spoken.

Religion. About two-thirds of the population of the
Sudan are Muslim. These people are concentrated in the
northern and central regions, which are almost completely
Muslim. Sudanese Islam falls generally within the Sunni experience, with the most common school of Islamic law being
the Maliki. However, there is a wide variety of religious
practice, with some "Muslim" communities still closely tied
to pre-Islamic customs, while others are quite thoroughly
Islamized. Further diversity is seen in the number of religious organizations. These range from individual or tribal
respect for a local religious teacher or family to membership
in one of the larger regional brotherhoods. The largest of
these, organized around prominent families, are the Ansar
(followers of the Mahdi and his descendants) and the tariqahs
like the Khatmiyyah.

There are an estimated half million Christians in the
Sudan. Most of these are in the south and they are divided
between Roman Catholic and Protestant, resulting from the
missionary activity of the past century. There are small
communities of Christians of other traditions, especially the
Coptic and other Middle Eastern churches, who came to the
Sudan originally as government officials, merchants, or teach-

ers in the days of Turco-Egyptian or British rule. There is no direct continuity between modern Sudanese Christians and the Christian kingdoms of the medieval Sudan.

The majority of Sudanese in the southern areas and in some northern areas like the Nuba Mountains, are neither Muslim nor Christian. They subscribe to local traditional African religions which are tied to the beliefs and customs of their ethnic units. In some areas practices have been modified by contact with Islam or Christianity, so that a clear distinction between these faiths and the local tradition may be difficult. Throughout the Sudan, pre-Christian and pre-Islamic customs have been continued to some extent so that distinctive Sudanese experiences have emerged within the framework of the larger religious traditions.

In general terms, religion, along with ethnic group and language, has been an important factor in individual and cultural identity in the Sudan.

EARLY HISTORY

The history of the Sudan is as diversified as its population. Unfortunately, at present much of Sudan's history is unknown or seen only dimly through the lens of oral and tribal tradition. The most information is available on the development of the central and northern areas in the Nile valley, but even there much remains to be learned. Recently much information has come from archeological efforts in Nubia to study sites before they were covered by the waters in the Aswan High Dam reservoir, Lake Nasser. Elsewhere in the Sudan many important sites remain to be studied. But the vigorous activity of the Sudan Department of Antiquities and other scholars means that new information is constantly being made available.

The Years B. C. Evidence of early human activity is scattered throughout the Sudan. Early Stone Age or Paleolithic sites suggest dates as early as 250,000 B. C. to some scholars. The most thoroughly studied sequences of early tool industries and settlement sites are in Nubia. There, around Wadi Halfa and now covered by Lake Nasser, for example, a series of cultures has been found with dates of perhaps 50,000 years ago. Local social evolution and the im-

migration of new peoples are both postulated as sources for gradual changes in Sudanese Paleolithic cultures.

The techniques of plant and animal domestication began to appear in the Sudan and by 4000 to 3000 B. C. the Shaheinab or Khartoum Neolithic culture in the central Sudan had emerged. Neolithic groups in the Sudan may have had relations with a wide range of cultures in north and northeast Africa. The closest affinities were with inhabitants of predynastic Egypt. What is known of the subsequent ancient history of the Sudan is closely tied to Egyptian history.

The modern study of ancient Sudanese history has been concentrated in Nubia where the building of dams has necessitated major archeological efforts to study sites before they were flooded. The first major salvage survey was begun in 1907 and directed by A. Reisner. This work made it possible to construct an outline of Nubian cultural history. Reisner used a simple terminological scheme which is still commonly used, naming the various cultures with a letter, so that the earliest one, related to predynastic and early dynastic Egypt, is called the A-Group and dates roughly around 3100-2600 B. C.

A-Group was independent but strongly influenced by emerging Egyptian civilization. Then, around 2500 B. C., the Egyptians conquered some of northern Nubia and local Sudanese culture changed. Reisner identified this as a special period, the time of the B-Group, but later scholars disagree on the degree of distinctiveness of the people of that time. As Egypt entered a period of disorganization, around 2160 B. C., Sudanese Nubia flourished. The C-Group and Kerma cultures emerged. They were influenced by Egypt but also had their own distinctive dynamism. This era came to an end when the revived Egypt of the New Kingdom conquered and established firm control over much of Nubia around 1500 B. C. The Egyptian viceroy of the province of Kush, as the area was called, held firm sway and Reisner's D-Group is simply Egyptian New Kingdom material located in the Sudan.

As the Egyptian Empire weakened, especially after 1100 B. C., Sudanese states again emerged with vigor and even became a refuge area for Egyptians fleeing civil war and foreign conquest. By 950 B. C. the Sudanese city of Napata had become the site of the major remaining temple of Amon, the god of the most important Egyptian priesthood. A distinctive Egyptian-Kushite culture evolved. Napata be-

came the capital of Kush and its kings even conquered Egypt
for a time, forming the 25th Dynasty after 750 B.C. When
the Assyrians conquered Egypt in 656 B.C., the Kushites
were driven back but maintained their independent Sudanese
state. The destruction of Napata by Psammetichus II, who
invaded from Egypt in 591 B.C., caused the capital to be
moved south to Meroe but did not destroy the state.

Meroe was a vibrant state influenced by Hellenistic
and Roman as well as ancient Egyptian ideas. However, it
developed its own cultural traits and may have been the gate-
way for Middle Eastern ideas and technologies into Africa.
Meroe began to meet pressures from growing states around
it, especially Axum in Ethiopia, and Meroe came to an end
around A.D. 350.

Medieval History. Little is known about Sudanese
history in the period of disorganization following the collapse
of Meroe. This is the time of the X-Group or Ballana culture, which was a post-Meroitic mixture of Roman, Kushite,
and new elements. Out of the confusion, three states emerged: Nobatia, Makuria, and Alwa. Their rulers converted
to Christianity between A.D. 543 and 580 and Nobatia and
Makuria merged into the kingdom of Dongola by 700.

The best-known aspect of the history of these states
is their relationship with Egypt, which became a part of the
new Islamic empire in 640. There were battles, treaties,
attacks, and counterattacks, with the long-term trend in fav-
or of the Muslims. Tradition says that the first Muslim became king of Dongola in 1315 and that Soba, the capital of
the last Christian kingdom, Alwa, fell in 1504. Scholars
now think that event may have taken place earlier. However,
relations were not all destructive. Arab Muslim tribes, merchants, and teachers gradually moved into the Sudan. They
intermarried, settled, and became Sudanese. As a result,
the end of the medieval Sudan was more a gradual transition
and conversion than an attack and conquest.

Post-Medieval/Pre-Modern Era. The three centuries
between the traditional date for the fall of Soba and the Turco-
Egyptian conquest of the Sudan in 1820-21 are of great importance in Sudanese history. The movement of new tribes and
the consolidation of institutions confirmed both the Islamization and the Arabization of much of the northern Sudan. Dur-

ing this time the modern pattern of tribal societies in the south was also being set. The major movements of the Nilotic tribes was completed and the Azande kingdoms were firmly established.

During this period it is possible to trace with more knowledge the main outlines of the history of the whole country, although much remains historically obscure to the modern observer. The best-known features relate to the emergence of a number of larger, regional states within the area of the modern Sudan.

The Funj sultanate was established in the central and northern Sudan early in the 16th century with its capital at Sennar. The origins of the Funj are still the subject of scholarly dispute. However, they probably were a non-Muslim, non-Arab group coming from the south or southeast. The state they established followed African patterns of kingship, although Islam rapidly became an important political force and the Funj converted. They defeated the earlier major Arab tribal state of the Abdallab and incorporated that group into the Funj political system as viceroys of the northern provinces. The Sultanate was the major force in the Nile valley and extended its control on occasion both east into the Red Sea hills and west into Kordofan.

The political system experienced a gradual evolution, with Islamization undermining the bases of the African kingship. In the late 17th century Sultan Badi II created a slave army and tensions developed, with the old Funj aristocracy feeling threatened. In 1720 the old nobility revolted and deposed the Sultan. Other revolts filled the century as groups broke away from control by Sennar. In 1761 a successful general, Muhammad Abu Likaylik, and his clan, the Hamaj, became the real rulers in Sennar, naming and deposing sultans. The final years of the sultanate were filled with internal conflict and the control of the Hamaj regents and their puppet rulers was increasingly restricted to the area around the capital. Tribal kingdoms emerged throughout the region and it was a divided and anarchic Sudan that the Turco-Egyptian forces invaded in 1820.

In Darfur in the western Sudan other sultanates were also emerging. Small states were created in medieval times and little is known of their history. The Daju gained control over part of the area before 1200 and were followed by the Tunjur. They were succeeded in turn by the Keira dynasty

which created a sultanate controlling most of Darfur from the mid-17th century until 1916. From the time of Sulayman So-long in the late 17th century, the Keira state was Islamic, although keeping many pre-Islamic features. The last of the Keira sultans was Ali Dinar, who was defeated by the British during World War I.

Islam was firmly established in the northern Sudan during the Funj and Keira periods. Traveling merchants and teachers opened the region to the rest of the Islamic world. Local schools were created and the great Islamic orders or tariqahs gained a firm foothold. Holy men and their families came to wield important influence in all areas of life. In this way the basic Sudanese Islamic patterns were set. They were focused around individuals in a personalized socioreligious order. The religious brotherhood joined the tribe and family as a primary basis for identity.

The period from the 15th to the 19th century was also of crucial importance in the development of the southern parts of the Sudan. It is during those centuries that tribal migra-tions brought the major groups to their modern locations and institutional structures were defined. The Nilotic peoples moved out of a cradleland in central Bahr al-Ghazal. The Dinka and Nuer moved a relatively short distance and their patterns of decentralized politico-tribal organization were con-firmed. Other wandering Nilotic groups also found their mod-ern homelands. Some were smaller and more isolated but those who settled on the White Nile in the Malakal-Fashoda area became the Shilluk. They developed a more centralized, monarchical tradition. The unity achieved under the king or "reth" enabled the Shilluk to preserve their tribal integrity in the face of outside attack in the 19th and 20th centuries.

The largest state to emerge in the south during this period was created by a non-Nilotic group, the Azande. These people, speaking a language of the Adamawa-Eastern subfamily of the Niger-Congo linguistic group, began to enter the southern Sudan in the 16th century. At first this move-ment had little cohesion and only created a pattern of small, scattered groupings. However, in the 18th century the Avun-gara arrived as a new wave of invaders and they were differ-ent. As a military aristocracy they succeeded in imposing their authority over the various Azande-speaking groups. The result was the creation of a well-organized and expanding state system. The key to expansion was the vigor and the rivalry of the royal princes who would leave the center and

carve out domains of their own. In this way internal division
was minimized and the weaker tribes in surrounding areas
were conquered and assimilated. This basic pattern was not
altered fundamentally until the British established control in
the 20th century.

Post-medieval experience created the foundations for
modern Sudanese society. The major states of both north
and south had provided more than simply tribal organization
and identity, although the tribal loyalty of the individual remained important. In the north the Islamization of society
was confirmed and its Arabization was far advanced. However, the geographical differences between north and south,
and sheer distance, meant that these factors had little influence in the south. There the major feature was the movement of peoples that brought the major tribes to their modern homelands. The period also saw the confirmation of decentralized political structures among most of the tribes, even
the large ones like the Dinka and Nuer, and the creation of
the special aristocratic empire of the Azande and the Shilluk
monarchy.

RECENT HISTORY

Turco-Egyptian Rule, 1820-1881. During the 19th
century a number of factors emerged which began to bring
these disparate peoples and regions together into a single
unit called the Sudan. Economic, religious, and political
organization broadened to countrywide activity at times, and
provided elements of integration which would coexist, and
sometimes conflict, with the elements of diversity.

In politics a dramatic change was brought about by
the conquest of much of the Sudan by Turco-Egyptian forces.
Muhammad Ali, the virtually independent Ottoman governor
of Egypt, decided to invade the region to his south. A variety of explanations are given for this: he hoped to pacify
troublesome elements along his southern border, he wanted
a source of gold and slaves, he wanted to create an empire
of his own. Whatever the reason, his army moved into the
Sudan under the command of his son, Ismail, in 1820. The
scattered tribal forces and the disintegrating Funj armies
were no match for the relatively modernized army from
Egypt. The central and northern areas of the Sudan were
quickly conquered.

In 1822 Ismail was murdered by a tribal chief in Shendi and a widespread revolt against the new conquerors followed. The opposition was soon crushed by the Turco-Egyptian forces who did not face another major local threat until the Mahdist movement in 1881. A civil and military administration was established with the capital in Khartoum. A bureaucratic structure emerged with provincial and district officers as well as central technical departments for such services as river steamers, posts, and telegraph. In this way a centralized, non-tribal governmental system was established and the modern political framework of the Sudan was begun.

The Turco-Egyptian rulers expanded the area under their control. By 1840 at least nominal control was won over the tribes of the Red Sea hills and the ports on the coast were gained. Expeditions to the south created at least a military presence, if not control, in much of that area. The final expansion was completed in 1874 with the conquest of Darfur.

Perhaps the most drastic changes were caused by the expansion of the slave trade during the 19th century. At first officially condoned, the trade destroyed many smaller tribes in the south and created a tradition of violent relations and mistrust between southern tribes and outsiders. Only the largest and best organized, or most isolated, tribes survived. The trade also created a group of powerful merchants with private armies. These people and those who profited with them became opposed to Egyptian rule when it attempted to limit and then abolish the slave trade.

By 1880 the Egyptian regime was growing unpopular. The administrative officials after mid-century were sometimes recruited from among Europeans and this was viewed unfavorably by local traditional Muslims. Even the Egyptians who were Muslims were often offensive to local opinion because they were more Europeanized or less religiously oriented than most Sudanese. The Egyptian officials often viewed posting in the Sudan as an unpleasant exile and some who came were corrupt and inefficient.

The Egyptians were able to secure the cooperation of some important local groups. Some tribes accepted the reality of the conquest very early and assisted the government. The Shayqiyyah tribe, for example, after strong but brief resistance, provided irregular cavalry for garrisons throughout

the Sudan.   A few tribal leaders, like the Abu Sinn family of the Shukriyyah, became important figures in the governmental structure itself.   Some religious teachers received training and help from the government in an effort to create religious leadership alternatives to the local teachers and orders.   The largest group to cooperate was the Khatmiyyah, a tariqah led by the Mirghani family.   Although this order was new to the Sudan, it had grown rapidly.

Many local religious leaders and tribes opposed Egyptian rule, although generally through noncooperation rather than by open revolt.   However, growing discontent reached a climax in the late 1870's.   The various opponents of the regime found an effective vehicle for expressing their discontent in the movement of Muhammad Ahmad, the Sudanese Mahdi.

The Mahdiyyah, 1881-1898.   Among those Sudanese distressed by what they believed to be the impiety of the Turco-Egyptian rulers was a religious man with a popular reputation for ascetic piety, Muhammad Ahmad ibn Abdallah. This man was initiated into the Sammaniyyah tariqah but had a dispute with his original teacher over the luxury of that person's life style.   Muhammad Ahmad lived as a recluse but attracted many followers.   He became convinced of the need to restore the purity of Islamic society and he believed himself to be the God-appointed guide, or mahdi, to bring about his final purification.   He toured the Sudan and then publically proclaimed his mission in 1881.

The government at first underestimated the scope of popular resentment and the potential popularity of the Mahdi. Forces sent to arrest the Mahdi were defeated and the momentum of revolt built rapidly.   As victory followed victory people flocked to the Mahdi's banner, and he soon controlled all of the northern Sudan but Wadi Halfa in the north and the Red Sea port of Suakin.   Charles Gordon had been sent to organize local resistance to the Mahdi and secure the evacuation of Egyptian forces and officials.   He became cut off in Khartoum and was killed in 1885 when the city fell after a long siege.

The Mahdi attempted to recreate the structures of the ...munity established by the Prophet Muhammad.   His followers were drawn from many different groups and they came to be called the Ansar.   The major elements in his move-

ment were drawn from the settled groups in the Nile valley,
many of whom were associated with the Mahdi's family, the
Baqqara tribesmen from the western Sudan, who were associated with the Mahdi's chief assistant, the Khalifah Abdallahi,
and the more isolated tribesmen of the eastern Sudan following Uthman Diqna and local religious leaders.

Soon after the fall of Khartoum, the Mahdi died. He
was succeeded by the Khalifah Abdallahi, who faced the difficult tasks of protecting the new state, consolidating the organization of the Mahdist movement, and keeping the diverse
factions of the movement unified. Between 1885 and 1898 the
Khalifah managed to defeat local revolts aroused by continuing messianic excitement and to control tension within the
movement between the Mahdi's family and their supporters
and his own tribal associates. He utilized some of the administrative structures of the Egyptian government and a relatively stable state was beginning to emerge in the 1890's.
The major threat to the Mahdist state was outside attack.
As Africa was partitioned among the European powers, Italy,
France, and Britain looked to the Sudan with interest. It
was the British who won, neutralizing Italian ambitions from
Eritrea and stopping the French at Fashoda. The British invaded the Mahdist state with an Anglo-Egyptian army which
faced fierce opposition, but won through its technological superiority. The last major battle was fought outside Omdurman in 1898.

During the Mahdist era the country-wide organization
of politics and economics had been continued and the Islamization of northern areas was further confirmed. At the same
time, the special identity of the Sudan as a separate country
had been emphasized. As a result, the Mahdi has been called by some "the first Sudanese nationalist".

The Anglo-Egyptian Sudan, 1899-1955. In 1899 an
Anglo-Egyptian agreement defined the new regime for the
Sudan. Devised by Lord Cromer, the British representative
in Egypt, it provided for an official Anglo-Egyptian control,
with flags of both countries flying side by side, and officials
drawn from both. The governor-general was to be appointed
by the Egyptian ruler on the recommendation of the British
government. In practice, the Sudan was controlled by the
British.

The organization of the new government relied on the

19th-century Turco-Egyptian precedents for central and provincial organization. At first most governors, inspectors, and officials were drawn from the Egyptian services. (Even many of the British in the Sudan were officers in the Egyptian Army on secondment.) However, a civil service recruited directly from British universities, and medical, veterinary, educational, and other services were soon created specifically for the Sudan.

The early years of British rule were mainly occupied with establishing control and maintaining order. In the north messianic movements continued to appear but were quickly put down. Mahdist writings and organizations were outlawed, but the Ansar continued in their adherence to Mahdism. Sayyid Abd al-Rahman al-Mahdi, a son of the Mahdi, provided the focus for Mahdist loyalties. However, since he was willing to cooperate with the British, especially in avoiding revolts during World War I, Mahdism ceased to be a threat to British-controlled public order by the 1920's. In the south there was also resistance, with many tribal revolts and much local reluctance. In all, more than 170 military patrols, each involving more than 50 men, were required in the first three decades of British rule to establish control. Sudanese resistance in the early years was almost completely tribal or traditional rather than nationalist or modern in style.

In economic terms the integration of the country continued. The transportation system was expanded, a new port-- Port Sudan--was built on the Red Sea, and plans were made for a large agricultural project in the Gezira. By the time of independence, there was considerable modern economic activity in the north, but little had been done to encourage modern economic development in the south.

The 1920's were important years of transition. By then the relatively limited educational development had created a small but articulate educated class in the Sudan. After early cooperation, this group began to be dissatisfied with their prospects and the lack of possibilities for self rule. With the emergence of the educated Sudanese, resistance to British rule and local definition of aspirations began to shift away from traditional and toward modern goals.

The educated group completed what was to become the triangle of local politics. One point was Sayyid Abd al-Rahman al-Mahdi with the Ansar and the other was Sayyid Ali al-Mirghani and the Khatmiyyah. The latter consistently

opposed Mahdism and had cooperated with the British. The Egyptians were the final factor. By 1930 various basic themes were emerging: Ansar-Khatmiyyah rivalry and their competition for educated support; the effort of the educated to create an effective nationalist movement while being forced to seek support from one or the other of the religious groups and one of the two interested outside governments; and the struggle between Britain and Egypt. The theater for working out these themes was primarily the northern Sudan. Increasingly the south was insulated by formal and informal British policies from developments in the north.

Initially both of the major religious leaders and the major tribal leaders cooperated with the British. Early nationalism found its expression in small, usually secret, organizations of educated Sudanese, like the Sudan Union Society (al-Ittihad) and the better-known White Flag League. Because of their anti-British tone, they gained some support from Egypt. The first phase came to a climax in 1924 when a series of demonstrations culminated in a military mutiny. The British were startled by the initial vigor of nationalism and reacted strongly, expelling most Egyptian officials from the Sudan and limiting the role of the educated Sudanese.

For the next two decades there was little overt national political activity. The British encouraged more traditional leaders, especially tribal, to take a more active role in government through a policy of "indirect rule." The two large religious groups were the most effectively organized mass associations in the country and their two leaders emerged as a focus for political action. The educated found that, even in their cultural organizations, the moment political choices like the election of officers arose, the groups became polarized along sectarian lines. In the early graduates-club, for example, two groups emerged: that of Shaykh Ahmad al-Sayyid al-Fil (the "Filists") with the support of Ali al-Mirghani, and the group around Muhammad Ali Shawqi (the "Shawqists") which had Abd al-Rahman al-Mahdi's sympathy. In addition to the sectarian division, sides were taken in the British-Egyptian rivalry, and the two competing slogans of Sudanese nationalism became either "Unity of the Nile Valley" or "Sudan for the Sudanese."

The educated Sudanese made an attempt to create a non-sectarian nationalist group in 1938 when they formed the Graduates Congress. However, the need for mass support soon caused the Congress leaders to turn to the Sayyids, and

the general growing desire for independence forced the choice
to be made between cooperating either with Britain or Egypt.

In terms of national growth the era leading up to party
politics at the end of World War II was filled with more than
partisan struggles.   Sudanese journalism emerged as a force
independent from the government.   Literature and literary
criticism prospered.   Two journals appeared which, though
short-lived, had an impact on the evolution of Sudanese intellectual life.   These were al-Nahdah, appearing in 1931-2,
and al-Fajr, which began publication in 1934 and later in the
decade became more actively political.   One of the arguments
at the time was whether or not there was such a thing as an
autonomous Sudanese culture.   The paradoxical nature of that
culture with both its profound ties to outside societies and its
distinctive character was debated.

The Graduates Congress gave impetus to intensified
political activity in 1942 by presenting a petition to the British
for speedy Sudanese self-government.   The abrupt rejection
of the Congress memorandum precipitated a split in that group.
The activists, whose leaders included Ismail al-Azhari, demanded a vigorous response and a policy of noncooperation
with the British.   This meant they came to be allied with
Egyptian nationalism and thus became proponents of Nile valley unity.   The activists formed their own political party, the
Ashiqqa, which was the first and most outspoken of a number
of parties supporting unity with Egypt.   The moderates in
Congress mistrusted the Egyptian aims and felt that independence might be more rapidly achieved by working with the
British.   As both groups sought mass support, they turned
to the religious organizations and nationalist politics became
sectarian, with Ali al-Mirghani and the Khatmiyyah giving
support to the unionists.   Abd al-Rahman al-Mahdi and the
Ansar worked with the more moderate nationalists in support
of a separate, independent Sudan, and they created the Mah-
dist-based Umma Party.

In this growing turmoil the British were also active,
trying to create instruments for controlling political developments.   An early step was the creation of the Advisory Council for the Northern Sudan in 1944.   The activists objected
because it had only advisory functions, excluded the southern
Sudan, and consisted largely of traditional leaders, so they
boycotted the Council.   The Legislative Assembly was formed
in 1948 and was an elected body including both northern and
southern representatives.   Unionists also boycotted it and the

Assembly was dominated by the Umma Party. In international terms, the Anglo-Egyptian stalemate over the British role in Egypt made agreement on the Sudan impossible. In the Sudan itself the basic pillars around which politics revolved were the opposing nationalist themes of unity or separate independence, the sectarian rivalries, and the struggle of the educated class to define its role more clearly.

The resolution came suddenly, with the key being the Egyptian Revolution in 1952. The new Egyptian leadership was more flexible regarding the Sudan and an agreement was signed in 1953 defining the steps toward Sudanese self-government and self-determination. Local politics were also made less confusing when most of the small unionist parties joined together, creating the National Unionist Party (NUP) led by Ismail al-Azhari. Elections for a new parliament were held late in 1953 and the NUP won a majority. The Umma Party also won a large number of seats and the only other large block of representatives was made up of southern members who were organized into the Liberal Party. Most of the smaller parties gradually disappeared.

Ismail al-Azhari became the first prime minister and under his leadership the Sudanization of the administration was rapidly completed. The NUP had supported a unity-of-the-Nile platform but political developments changed perspectives. As the Sudan moved toward the time of self-determination, the pro-unity people became convinced of the viability of a separately independent Sudan. Independence was voted by the NUP-led parliament and on January 1, 1956, the British withdrew and the Sudan became an independent state. One cloud had arisen on the horizon in 1955. Southerners were upset by the limited role given them in the Sudanization of the government and they feared northern domination. Rumors and mistrust spread in the south. In August 1955 a mutiny broke out among southern army troops in Equatoria. Many people were killed and a number of southern soldiers fled into exile. The issue of integrating the south into the independent Sudan became a major problem.

INDEPENDENCE

The Sudan inherited a parliamentary structure from the Anglo-Egyptian regime, but the political system had little stability. Old cleavages and new problems emerged during the first two years of independence. The economic situation

was troublesome, with the Sudan having difficulty marketing
its cotton, its major export.   The issues relating to what the
permanent form of the political system should be--parliamen-
tary or presidential, centralized or federalist--were never
resolved to the satisfaction of the major political forces.
The problem of the south remained unsolved and southern
leaders began to withdraw in discouragement.   Finally, even
among the northern politicians the minimum consensus for
effective government was not achieved, with politics becoming
little more than an arena for personal, factional, and sectarian feuds.

The political forces which interacted after independence
were continuations of earlier groups.   The activist, educated
Sudanese, with solid support in the more modernized urban
areas, generally looked to Ismail al-Azhari for leadership,
although small radical groups existed, especially the well-
organized Sudanese Communist Party.   The Khatmiyyah under the leadership of Ali al-Mirghani had joined with al-Azhari in the formation of the NUP.   This alliance soon broke
and in 1956 Sayyid Ali's followers formed the People's Democratic Party (PDP).   The Ansar, following Abd al-Rahman
al-Mahdi, continued to be the mainstay of the Umma Party.

When the PDP was formed, a major reversal in Sudanese politics took place.   Until 1956 the Mahdi-Mirghani
rivalry had been strong enough for the Khatmiyyah, though
quite conservative, to ally themselves with the more radical
Sudanese nationalists.   However, the tensions between Khatmiyyah leadership and al-Azhari which led to the break-up
of the NUP also led to a PDP-Umma alliance, pitting the
traditional religious forces against al-Azhari and the NUP.
The PDP-Umma cooperation created a coalition government
with Abdallah Khalil (Umma) as prime minister and put al-
Azhari into opposition.   Since the Umma and PDP agreed
on little more than opposition to al-Azhari, the effectiveness
of governmental policy formation suffered.   After new elections in 1958 failed to clarify the political picture, and the
economic situation grew worse, the army chief of staff, Ibrahim Abboud, took control of the government through a military coup in November 1958.

It is believed by many that both the PDP and Umma
received the coup willingly.   However, Abboud made parties
illegal and the Ansar soon lost most of the influence they had
within the military regime.   Ali al-Mirghani, who was never
as directly active in politics as the Mahdist family, was able

to maintain contact with the Abboud group although the PDP
was outlawed along with the other parties. Northern politicians became restive and some were jailed briefly. It was
the southern leadership that suffered the most. The Abboud
government attempted to "solve" the southern question militarily. This turned a bad situation into a major civil war.
By the end of the Abboud era in 1964 most southern leaders
were either in exile, prison, or fighting openly against the
Khartoum government. Southern resistance had become organized into a guerrilla movement, the Anya Nya, and a number of political organizations in exile.

Repression, lack of imagination, inability to handle
the southern problem, and other factors created widespread
discontent with the Abboud regime. In October 1964 student
demonstrations, strikes, brave resistance by professional and
legal leaders, and other activities forced the removal of the
military regime. It was replaced by a transitional government led by Sirr al-Khatim al-Khalifah. Radical educated
groups had an influential role in the new civilian government
because of their prominent role in the October Revolution.
However, as elections and parliamentary government again
developed, the older parties regained control.

By 1965 the balance of political forces was different,
although the actors were familiar. The radical intelligentsia
was actively represented, especially in the small but effective
Communist Party. They had few seats in parliament but influenced at least the tone of political rhetoric. The NUP reemerged under al-Azhari and proved again to be a good vote
winner. The PDP's position was less clear. It allied itself
for a time with the Communists and boycotted elections. As
a result, for a while its position was rather insecure. Ali
al-Mirghani's health and age made him less active in national
affairs so that Khatmiyyah leadership was less concentrated
than before, although it maintained cohesion even after his
death in 1968.

The leading party in the elections following the revolution was the Umma, benefitting from the continued mass
tribal loyalty of the Ansar. The problem facing the Mahdists
was a split in the Mahdist family leadership. Abd al-Rahman
had died in 1959 and his experienced son and successor,
Siddiq, died unexpectedly in 1961. Ansar leadership roles
were divided. Siddiq's son Sadiq became the head of the
Umma Party, while al-Hadi, a more conservative son of
Abd al-Rahman, became the _imam_ or religious leader of the
Ansar.

In parliament following the revolution, the Umma and NUP formed a coalition. Muhammad Ahmad Mahjub (Umma) became prime minister, while al-Azhari gained the post of president of the Supreme Council, which legally functioned as head of state. Divisions soon appeared among the Ansar as the Oxford-educated and more modern Sadiq disagreed with the more traditional Imam al-Hadi. This dispute carried over into politics as Mahjub tended to support al-Hadi. Sadiq engineered the ousting of the Mahjub-Imam wing of his party from power and became prime minister himself in 1966-1967. A reconciliation between Sadiq and the Imam brought Mahjub back into office but by then it seemed clear to many Sudanese that the old pattern of personal and factional bickering had returned to dominate politics. This was perhaps only emphasized by the reunion of two bitter rivals, al-Azhari's NUP and the PDP, into the Democratic Unionist Party in 1969.

The ineffectiveness of the parliamentary regime in dealing with the southern problem also created discontent. Its solution had been a high priority matter for the civilians who overthrew Abboud. An important step was taken in 1965 when many southern leaders returned from exile for a Round Table Conference. However, southern divisions and northern inflexibility proved to be major stumbling blocks. As northern factional politics reemerged, leaders in Khartoum reverted to the attempt to solve the problem militarily and the war continued.

By May 1969 the feeling of unrest paved the way for a group of younger soldiers, led by Ja'far Numayri, to take over the government. The old parties were declared illegal, a Revolutionary Command Council was set up, and a new cabinet including younger and independent civilians was formed. The May Revolution saw itself as a continuation of the October Revolution. Its leaders adopted domestic socialist programs and aimed at curbing conservative elements in Sudanese politics. Finding a solution to the southern question was announced as a major goal.

The Numayri revolutionary government has faced a wide variety of challenges, but has also worked to create a new political structure for the Sudan which would avoid the problems of the old system. Initially, although the Revolutionary Command Council (RCC) was the real center of power, the more civilian cabinet had an important role in the operation of the government. Then more formal political

institutions were created.   In May 1971 the Sudanese Socialist
Union (SSU) was formed as a mass organization to replace
political parties.   In January 1972 the first SSU congress approved a national charter and also the basic outline for a
permanent constitution.   After extensive discussions, this
constitution was formally promulgated in May 1973 and a new
government was formed under President Numayri.

Dealing with the southern question was a key element
in the constitutional development.   The northern insistence
on a centralized political system had been an obstacle since
the achievement of independence.   The early announcement
by the RCC that it recognized southern autonomy was an important step.   In addition, the evolution of southern leadership also helped to pave the way for a settlement.   In the
1960's a large number of short-lived southern political organizations had made southern unity of action difficult.   However,
in 1969 much of the southern resistance, especially the military activities in the Sudan itself, became effectively coordinated by Joseph Lagu.   With relatively unified southern leadership, more effective negotiations were possible.   Early in
1972 northern and southern negotiators met in Addis Ababa
and created a peace agreement which was formally signed late
in March.   Both sides were able to make the cease-fire effective and in a surprisingly short time the northern and southern military and administrative systems were integrated.
There have been some incidents but in mid-1977 the basic
outlines of the settlement were still in force.

Regional autonomy for the south was recognized in the
permanent constitution.   A broader decentralization of government in general has been a stated goal of the Numayri regime.   The hope is to create structures which would encourage popular participation without losing the benefits of centralized efficiency in planning.   One of the continuing series of
efforts in this direction was the reorganization of provincial
government, changing from a system of a few large provinces
to one having a greater number of smaller ones.

The Numayri regime has also shown an evolution in
economic approach.   The first months were rather disorgan-
ized but soon a more extensive socialism was instituted:
there was the nationalization of banks (May 1970), cotton
marketing (June 1970), and all newspapers (August 1970).
However, especially after disagreements with the radical
left, there was a feeling that the expansion of the government's economic role had been too rapid and there was some
loosening of early control measures.

In political terms the revolutionary government was seen initially as a more radical regime. Members of the Communist Party and officers sympathetic to the party were active and influential. The first real challenge came from conservative forces, especially the Ansar. The Imam al-Hadi led an open revolt in March 1970 and was quickly defeated. Organized conservative opposition within the Sudan was crushed and Ansar leadership and other groups, like the Muslim Brotherhood, began to work in exile. In the next year Numayri worked to avoid moving too far to the left and began to clash with the Communists. This reached a climax in July 1971 when a coup led by leftist officers took control of Khartoum for three days. When Numayri regained control he began a campaign to crush the opposition from the left. Those leftist leaders who avoided execution were forced underground or into exile. Thus, the major opposition to the Numayri government has come, and continued through 1977 to come, from both ends of the political spectrum--those who think he is too radical and those who think he is not radical enough.

PRESENT GOVERNMENT/ECONOMICS

The Sudan is defined in its constitution as a democratic republic. The central government is still the basic focus of political power and policy making. A single mass political organization, the Sudanese Socialist Union, is the legal basis for popular participation in politics.

In addition, important steps have been taken in the direction of decentralization, especially in the establishment of regional autonomy for the southern provinces. There is a High Executive Council (or cabinet) for the Southern Region that has some power to determine action on the local and regional level. For regional and local administration, in the entire country there are 18 provinces.

Economically the Sudan is primarily agricultural. Many Sudanese still work within the traditional, subsistence sector, but a modern agricultural sector also exists. The core of this is the Gezira Scheme, which was established as a major cotton growing area during the 1920's and is one of the most successful large-scale schemes in Africa. In the 1970's there has been considerable investment in agricultural development, with some seeing the Sudan as the future "breadbasket of the Arab world."

THE DICTIONARY

A-GROUP. The name given to the local Nubian culture contemporary with Pre-Dynastic and Early Dynastic Egypt,
i.e., 3100-2600 B.C. There are affinities of a physical
and cultural nature between the two societies. Some authorities see an abrupt end to A-Group culture with an
Egyptian invasion and replacement by the B-Group culture
(q.v.), while others see continuity and the gradual development of new elements.

ABA ISLAND. An island in the White Nile near Kosti. It
was the religious center of Muhammad Ahmad al-Mahdi
(q.v.) and was the center of the Mahdi family's agricultural holdings in the 20th century as well as being the
religio-political center for the Ansar (q.v.).

ABABDA. A nomadic tribe with some sedentary sections in
upper Egypt and the northern Sudan. They are largely
Arabic-speaking, although they are believed to be of
Beja (q.v.) origin. They were traditionally important as
the guardians of the caravan routes from Korosko to Abu
Hamed. They served as irregulars in the Egyptian army
in the 19th century, aiding in the initial conquest and in
fighting against the Mahdist movement.

ABBADI, BASHIR. Minister of Communications in the first
Sudan Socialist Union government in 1971. He remained
in that post through many changes of cabinet into 1976.
In 1976 he was named Assistant Secretary General for
Ideology and Development in the Sudan Socialist Union
and was appointed to the Political Bureau of the SSU.

ABBAS, KHALID HASAN. A member of the original Revolutionary Command Council of the May Revolution (1969).
He served as Minister of Defense, Commander in Chief
of the armed forces, and Vice President. His support
was important in the restoration of the Numayri regime
after a brief revolution in July, 1971. He resigned all

25

his posts in 1972 but was appointed presidential advisor
on African affairs in 1975 and became Minister of Health
in 1976. He is believed to advocate policies of strong
Sudanese cooperation with Egypt.

ABBAS, MEKKI, 1911- . Educated in Gordon College and
England, he served in the Ministry of Education (1931-
1946) and was active in bodies leading to Sudanese self-
government like the Advisory Council for the Northern
Sudan (q. v.). He edited a small but influential news-
paper after World War II and wrote an important study,
The Sudan Question. After 1958 he worked outside the
Sudan in international agencies and in the mid-1960's he
was Assistant Director General of the United Nations
Food and Agricultural Organization.

ABBOUD, IBRAHIM, 1900- . Sudanese soldier and Prime
Minister (1958-1964). He was educated in Gordon College and the Khartoum Military College, entering the
Sudan Defense Force in 1925. He served in many areas
in World War II and was promoted to General in 1954.
He was commander in chief of the armed forces after
independence and took control of the government in a
military coup in November, 1958. He was President of
the Supreme Council of the Armed Forces, Prime Minister, and the leading figure in the military government
of 1958-1964. He was forced to resign and retire as a
result of the October Revolution of 1964.

ABD AL-HALIM, AHMAD. Sudanese political leader active
in government affairs after the 1969 Revolution, serving
in the SSU Political Bureau since 1972. In 1975 he was
named Minister of Information and Culture and in 1976
he became the Speaker of the People's Assembly.

ABD AL-MAHMUD, FATMA. Sudanese political leader.
She was named to the newly created post of Minister of
State for Social Welfare in 1975 and became Minister of
Social Affairs in 1976. Active in SSU affairs, she was
also named secretary of the SSU Women's Committee in
1976.

ABD AL-MAJID, YAHYA. Sudanese political leader. He is
a long standing member of cabinets in the Numayri revolutionary regime. He was named Minister of Irrigation
in 1971 and retained that position into 1976, through a
number of cabinet changes.

ABD AL-MUN'IM MUHAMMAD, 1896-1946. Sudanese business man. He formed a large import-export firm early
in the 20th century. He was a founder of Printing and
Publishing Company, Ltd., publisher of al-Nīl newspaper,
associated with Ansar (q.v.) interests. He was an early
member of the Graduates Congress (q.v.).

ABD AL-QADIR WAD HABUBA, d.1908. A religious revolutionary. He was an active follower of the Mahdi.
After the fall of the Mahdist state he returned to his
home in the Blue Nile area. Continuing religious fervor
and local land ownership disputes caused him to lead a
revolt in 1908 against British control. Although his
movement was quickly crushed and he was executed, the
revolt pointed up the continuing potential for religious
uprisings of a Mahdist nature.

ABD AL-RAHMAN, ALI, 1904- . Sudanese politician. He
was a judge in the Islamic religious courts until he was
elected to parliament in 1953 as a member of the NUP.
He was closely associated with the Khatmiyyah (q.v.)
leadership and became president of the PDP when it was
formed in 1956. He served in many cabinets--Minister
of Justice (1954-5), Minister of Education (1955-6), Minister of Interior (1956-8), Minister of Agriculture (1958).
After the 1964 Revolution he was again president of the
PDP and became Vice President of the DUP formed by
the PDP-NUP merger in 1967. His political activity
came to an end with the 1969 revolution.

ABD AL-RAHMAN WAD AL-NUJUMI, d.1889. Mahdist commander and early follower of the Mahdi. He was out-
standing among the Ansar officers for military skill.
He commanded the major attempt to invade Egypt and
was killed when his army was defeated at Toski in 1889.

ABDALLAB. An Arab group descended from a 15th-century
leader, Abdallah Jammā'. They controlled the area
around the confluence of the Niles and may have conquered the capital of Alwa (q.v.). They were defeated
by Amara Dunqas (q.v.) and became the hereditary viceroys over northern Funj lands, bearing the title manjil
(q.v.). Their residence was in Qarri until late in the
18th century, when they moved to Halfayat al-Muluk.
The Abdallab gained virtual independence in the last
years of the Funj but were hard pressed in the wars of
the era by the Hamaj (q.v.) and others. They are now
scattered in the central and Blue Nile areas.

ABDALLAH DAFA'ALLAH AL-'ARAKI see ARAKIYYIN

ABDALLAH JAMMĀ', d. ca. 1560. Arab tribal leader who
succeeded in conquering the central riverain lands and
establishing a capital at Qarri. He was defeated by
Amara Dunqas (q. v.) at Arbaji but was given a post of
special distinction in the new Funj (q. v.) state. Abdallah, and his descendants, the Abdallab (q. v.) were the
viceroys over the northern Funj lands.

ABDALLAHI AL-TA'ISHI (1846-1899). Successor to Muhammad Ahmad al-Mahdi (q. v.), and commonly known as
"the Khalifah," He was from a family of religious notables among the Ta'isha, a Baqqara (q. v.) tribe in Darfur. He believed that the time of the mahdi (q. v.) was
at hand and travelled in search of this figure. He met
and became a disciple of Muhammad Ahmad and was an
early enthusiast in the Mahdist mission. As a compe-
tant organizer and commander he became the most important assistant to the Mahdi. He was named successor,
or khalifah, and assumed control of the movement on the
Mahdi's death in 1885. He thus became the ruler of the
northern Sudan. He was able to create a relatively ef-
ficient administrative structure but his methods were often harsh. He faced internal revolt and external attack
but managed to keep control through increasing reliance
upon his relatives and the Baqqara tribesmen. His state
fell in the face of the Anglo-Egyptian invasion which culminated in the Battle of Omdurman in 1898. The Khalifah was killed a few months later in a last battle at
Umm Dibaykarat.

ABU AL-KAYLIK see MUHAMMAD ABU LIKAYLIK

ABU HASSABO, ABD AL-MAJID. Sudanese politician in the
NUP. He held a number of cabinet posts in the period
of party politics following the 1964 Revolution. He was
an important figure in NUP decision making. After the
1969 Revolution he was tried and convicted of misuse of
funds and was jailed. After release in 1975 he was accused by the Numayri regime of involvement in various
coup attempts.

ABU ISSA, FARUK. Sudanese lawyer and politician. He
was a member of the Communist Party of the Sudan
(q. v.) Executive Committee and was active in the 1964
Revolution. After the 1969 Revolution he was active in

various cabinets serving, at times, as Minister of Labor
and Foreign Affairs. He was part of the CPS group that
worked closely with the Numayri regime and opposed the
CPS leadership of Abd al-Khaliq Mahjub (q.v.).

ABU JOHN. A southern Sudanese soldier of Zande origin.
He was British trained and was active in southern resistance in the late 1960's. After the Addis Ababa Agreement of 1972 (q.v.) he was integrated into the Sudanese
Army.

ABU LIKAYLIK   see   MUHAMMAD ABU LIKAYLIK

ABU RANNAT, MUHAMMAD AHMAD, 1905- . Sudanese
judge. He was educated at Gordon College and the
School of Law (Khartoum). He served in various legal
and judicial posts, becoming a Judge of the High Court
(1950-5) and then Chief Justice of the Sudan (1955-64).
He had influence during the regime of Ibrahim Abboud
(q.v.), devising the Local Council system, and was important in the legal transition involved in the 1964 Revolution. After that he acted on a number of international
legal bodies.

ABU RA'UF GROUP. A literary and nationalist discussion
group in the 1920's and 1930's composed of younger graduates. Members of the group were active in the formation of the Graduates Congress (q.v.) in 1938. They
tended to be more militantly nationalist than the other
"literary" groups, like the Hashmab (q.v.). Among the
prominent members were Hamad Tawfiq Hamad (q.v.)
and Khidr Hamad (q.v.).

ABU SINN, AHMAD AWAD AL-KARIM, ca. 1790-1870. Leader of the Shukriyyah tribe in the 19th century and member of the Abu Sinn family (q.v.). He was an important
advisor to the Turco-Egyptian rulers and was one of the
few local notables to gain high rank in their regime. He
served as governor of Khartoum (1860-70) and had authority over the nomad tribes between the White Nile and
Ethiopia.

ABU SINN, MUHAMMAD AHMAD HARDALLU, 1830-1917.
Leader of the Shukriyyah tribe and a son of Ahmad Awad
al-Karim Abu Sinn (q.v.). He was a recognized tribal
leader under the Turco-Egyptian government, joined the
Mahdist movement, and was a Shukriyyah leader during

the Anglo-Egyptian regime. He was a poet whose works
gained wide acceptance in the Sudan.

ABU SINN FAMILY. The leading family of the Shukriyyah
tribe (q. v.). The traditional founder of the family is
Sha'a al-Din, who lived in the 16th century. However,
the family and tribe gained importance only in the 18th
and 19th centuries under the leadership of Awad al-
Karim and his son, Ahmad (q. v.). They gained a strong
position in the warfare at the end of the Funj era. Then
Ahmad Abu Sinn became an ally of the Turco-Egyptian
regime and his family and tribe became dominant in the
central part of the country. The Abu Sinns tried to remain aloof from the Mahdist movement and suffered from
famine and fighting in the last quarter of the century.
During the 20th century the family again had a position
of influence as major tribal notables. After World War
II members of the Abu Sinn family were active in politics, working in the Socialist Republican Party (q. v.)
and the NUP, and later the PDP. Members of the family have been elected to parliaments and assemblies and
have served occasionally in cabinets. The family continues to have some influence and has been represented
in the assemblies formed after the 1969 revolution.

ABU ZAYD, MAMOUN AWAD. Sudanese political leader.
He was a member of the Revolutionary Council of the
1969 Revolution and served in the early cabinets. He
was named the Secretary General of the SSU when it was
formed in 1971 and served in that post for a year. In
1975 he was appointed to the SSU Political Bureau and
became Minister of Interior in 1976. He is believed to
support policies of close Sudanese-Egyptian cooperation.

ADAMAWA-EASTERN. A subfamily of the Niger-Congo linguistic group, whose major representative in the Sudan
is the Azande (q. v.).

ADDIS ABABA AGREEMENT OF 1972. This is the agreement between the Sudanese Government and southerners
which created a settlement to the war in the southern
Sudan. It granted amnesty and provided for substantial
southern regional autonomy.

ADVISORY COUNCIL FOR THE NORTHERN SUDAN. (ACNS)
The ACNS was created by the British to provide a channel for expression of Sudanese opinion. It had only ad-

visory powers but was a formal step toward self-government. Its first session was in 1944 and it was dissolved
with the creation of the Legislative Assembly (q.v.) in
1948.

ADWOK, LUIGI, 1929- . Southern Sudanese politician of
Shilluk origin. He was elected to Parliament in 1958.
After the 1964 Revolution he was on the Executive Committee of the Southern Front (q.v.) and was their representative in the Supreme Council of State (1964-5). He
left the Front and was elected to Parliament in 1967.
After the 1969 Revolution he served in the cabinet for a
time as Minister of Public Works (1971) and then in the
Southern Region High Executive Council created by the
Addis Ababa Agreement of 1972 (q.v.). He served for
two years (1974-6) in the SSU Political Bureau. He was
originally a schoolmaster, educated at the Bakht Er Ruda
Institute of Education.

AFRICAN NATIONAL FRONT see NILE PROVISIONAL
GOVERNMENT

AHMAD, JAMAL MUHAMMAD, 1917- . Sudanese diplomat
and scholar. He was educated in University College,
Exeter, and Oxford. His scholarly writings include The
Intellectual Origins of Egyptian Nationalism. He served
in the Sudanese Foreign Ministry, acting as ambassador
to Iraq (1956-9), Ethiopia (1959-64), United Nations (1965-
7), and Great Britain (1969). He served as Foreign Minister in the Numayri era (1975-6) and in other foreign
affairs-related posts.

AHMAD, MUHAMMAD AL-BAQIR. Sudanese political leader
and soldier. He was named Minister of Interior in the
first SSU cabinet in 1971 and held that position at various
times in the following years. In 1972 he was named
First Vice President and remained in that post into 1976.

AHMAD AL-TAYYIB IBN BASHIR see SAMMANIYYAH

AHMAD IBN IDRIS, 1760-1837. A religious teacher who
influenced the Sudan through his students. He was born
in Morocco and taught in Arabia. His ideas of Islamic
revival and of using tariqahs (q.v.) as instruments of
that revival inspired a number of religious leaders important in the Sudan. These include Muhammad Uthman
of the Mirghani family (q.v.), Muhammad al-Sughayyir

of the Majdhubiyyah (q. v.), Ibrahim al-Rashid of the Rashidiyyah (q. v.), and his own family who led the Idrisiyyah (q. v.).

AHMAD MUMTAZ PASHA, ca. 1825-1874. An officer in the Turco-Egyptian army and administration in the 19th century. He is best known for having initiated largescale cultivation of cotton in the Sudan. He was briefly governor-general but was accused of corruption and died soon after his dismissal.

AHRAR see LIBERAL PARTY (Hizb al-Ahrar)

AKOBO INCIDENT (MARCH 1975). A mutiny of some southern troops at Akobo in Upper Nile Province. The cause was minor but indicated the continuing potential for unrest in the south.

AL- The definite article in Arabic. To find a word beginning with "al-", look under the word following it. For example, to find "al-Mahdi" ("the Mahdi") look under "Mahdi. "

ALI ABD AL-LATIF. A Sudanese nationalist leader in the 1920's. He was an army officer of Dinka origin who was dismissed for political reasons. At first he advocated Sudanese independence, through his own Sudan United Tribes Association, for which he was jailed briefly in 1922. This gave him some fame and, on his release in 1923 he worked to create the White Flag League advocating union with Egypt. He was involved in the demonstrations in 1924 and was again jailed.

ALI DINAR IBN ZAKARIYA IBN MUHAMMAD FADL, ca. 1865-1916. The last sultan of Darfur, ruling from 1898-1916. As a young man he participated in anti-Mahdist revolts in Darfur and then cooperated briefly with the Mahdist regime. At the time of the Anglo-Egyptian conquest he eliminated his rivals and received British recognition as sultan. He ruled relatively effectively in Darfur but during World War I he renounced allegiance to Anglo-Egyptian rule. He was killed in 1916 during a skirmish following the total defeat of his army by a British force.

ALI WAD HILU, d. 1899. A Mahdist commander. He was named by the Mahdi as one of his four khalifahs (q. v.).

He was killed along with the Khalifah Abdallahi (q.v.) in the last battle of the Mahdiyyah in 1899.

ALIER, ABEL, 1933- . Sudanese political leader and lawyer of Dinka origin. He studied law in Khartoum and London. He was an active member of the Southern Front (q.v.) from its beginning in 1964. He was elected to parliament (1968-9) and has continuously held posts of cabinet rank since the 1969 Revolution, serving as Minister of Housing (1969), Supply (1969-70), Public Works (1970-1), Southern Affairs (1971). In 1971 he was named a vice president of the country and represented the Sudanese Government in the negotiations leading up to the Addis Ababa Agreement of 1972 (q.v.). In addition to his post as 2nd Vice President, which he retained into 1976, he was named president of the newly created Southern Region High Executive Council.

ALWA. A kingdom which emerged in the central Sudan after the fall of Meroe. Its capital was at Soba near modern Khartoum. The rulers were converted to Monophysite Christianity by Longinus (q.v.) around A.D. 580 and Alwa survived as a Christian state longer than the Nubian kingdoms to the north. According to tradition, Soba finally fell to the Funj (q.v.) in 1504, although the kingdom may have collapsed before then.

AMARA DUNQAS. The founder of the Funj Sultanate (q.v.) of Sennar, ruling from 1504 to 1534. Leading the Funj, probably a southern Nubian people whose homeland was on the upper White Nile, he created the city of Sennar in 1504 and became the first ruler since ancient times to unite the riverain Sudan north of the equatorial swamps. The state he built was a federation of local rulers under Funj overlordship. Amara may have originally been pagan or Christian but Funj rulers were Muslim by 1523.

AMIN, NAFISA AHMAD al-. Sudanese political leader. She was named Deputy Minister for Youth and Sport in the first SSU cabinet, formed in 1971. She was the first Sudanese woman to attain a government office of this rank.

AMIN MUHAMMAD AL-AMIN, al- see GEZIRA TENANTS UNION

AMINA BINT FATIMA see AWLAD JABIR

ANGLO-EGYPTIAN AGREEMENT OF 1953. This agreement outlined the steps to be taken for Sudanese self-rule and self-determination. It provided the basis for the parliamentary elections of 1953 and the first Sudanese cabinet, formed by Ismail al-Azhari (q.v.).

ANGLO-EGYPTIAN SUDAN. The name for the area of the current Democratic Republic of the Sudan during the period 1899-1955. The regime was defined by the Anglo-Egyptian Agreement of 1899 and was often called the Condominium (q.v.). In theory both Egypt and Great Britian participated in ruling the Sudan at this time, but, in practice, it was the British who ruled.

ANGLO-EGYPTIAN TREATY OF 1936. This treaty redefined Anglo-Egyptian relations in light of the development of Egyptian nationalism. The Sudan was covered in an article which reaffirmed the existing administrative arrangements and opened the way for a little more Egyptian participation in administering the Sudan. The British and Egyptians promulgated this treaty without consulting any Sudanese. This helped to arouse nationalist feelings in the Sudan and was a factor in the creation of the Graduates Congress (q.v.).

ANSAR. The Arabic term for "helpers" which was applied to some of the early companions of the Prophet Muhammad. In the Sudan the term applies to the followers of Muhammad Ahmad al-Mahdi (q.v.) and his descendants.

ANTI-IMPERIALIST FRONT. A party formed in 1953 which acted as the public vehicle for the then-clandestine Communist Party of the Sudan (q.v.). The Front's president was Hasan Tahir Zarruq (q.v.) and its leftist viewpoints appealed to some of the educated Sudanese. It won one parliamentary seat in 1953 and participated in various commissions, such as the National Constitutional Commission of 1956. In 1957 it joined the anti-Umma alliance called the National Front (q.v.). It urged its supporters to vote for NUP (q.v.) candidates in the 1958 elections and ceased to operate as a legal entity after the Abboud coup in November 1958.

ANUAK. A group of Nilotes (q.v.) primarily located near the Ethiopian highlands, with many living in Ethiopia. In contrast to most other Nilotes, they are cultivators and herders of sheep and goats rather than relying mainly

on cattle herding. Through use of firearms they were
able to mount substantial resistance to the British early
in the 20th century and were not subdued until 1920-1.

ANYA NYA. Southern guerrilla military organization formed
in 1963. It was related to SANU (q.v.) but became a
virtually autonomous military organization operating within the Sudan. As southern politicians in exile were unable to create a unified resistance movement, Anya Nya
leaders became increasingly active in political affairs.
Finally, in 1969 the Anya Nya commander, Joseph Lagu,
succeeded in bringing together various factions in the
South Sudan Liberation Movement (SSLM). Under Lagu
the SSLM was a principal agent in negotiating the 1972
settlement of the southern conflict. After the Addis Ababa Agreement of 1972 (q.v.), Anya Nya soldiers were
integrated into the Sudanese army and government services.

ANYIDI REVOLUTIONARY GOVERNMENT (ARG). A southern
political group. It was formed in 1969 as a result of a
split within the Nile Provisional Government (q.v.).
The ARG was led by Emidio Tafeng, a commander in
the Anya Nya (q.v.). The ARG became a part of the
Southern Sudan Liberation Movement in 1970.

ARAB. About one-third of the Sudanese are "Arabs." The
term is used in a variety of ways. It can refer to descendants of tribes coming from the Arabian Peninsula
for more than a millenium; it can also refer to cultural
characteristics or people who speak Arabic, regardless
of their ancestry. Traditional genealogies identify most
Sudanese Arabs as either in the Juhayna group (q.v.) or
the Jaaliyyin (q.v.).

ARAB FUND FOR ECONOMIC AND SOCIAL DEVELOPMENT
(AFESD). A Kuwait-based financing organization with
investments in the Sudan.

ARAKIYYIN. A holy family with influence centered in the
Blue Nile area. The traditional founder of the family
was Abdallah Dafa'allah al-'Araki. He lived around 1570
and was one of the first khalifahs (q.v.) in the Sudan of
the Qadiriyyah (q.v.). Around 1800 some leaders of the
clan switched to the Sammaniyyah (q.v.). Many Arakiyyin fled from Turco-Egyptian rule, returning gradually
in the 19th century. The tomb of the founder and its

custodian-patrons maintain local religious prestige in Abu Haraz.

ASHIGGA (ashiqqa or "blood brothers"). A major political party in the post-World War II period. It was formed by militant nationalists within the Graduates Congress (q. v.). They had controlled the Congress executive committee by 1943 and formed a separate party in 1944 under the leadership of Ismail al-Azhari (q. v.). The party supported unity with Egypt and opposed official cooperation with the British. The Ashigga received the support of Ali al-Mirghani (q. v.) and the Khatmiyyah (q. v.). The influence of the party began to decline by 1949-50 when much Khatmiyyah support went to the newly-formed National Front (q. v.) and British-sponsored, elected assemblies gained more popular recognition. The party itself split into two factions. A dissident group led by Muhammad Nur al-Din (q. v.) opposed al-Azhari and his supporters. The party was dissolved when both factions joined the National Unionist Party (q. v.) in 1952. Ashigga politics and leadership continued to be an important force within the NUP.

ATTA, HASHIM al-. Sudanese soldier and political leader. He was a member of the original Council of the Revolution for the 1969 Revolution and served in early cabinets. He was dismissed from his civil and military posts in November, 1970. In July, 1971, he participated in the short-lived coup and was executed.

AVUNGARA see AZANDE

AWADALLAH, BABIKR, 1917- . Sudanese judge and political leader. After studying law in Khartoum and London he served as a lawyer and district judge. He resigned to become Speaker of the House of Representatives in Parliament (1954-7) and then rejoined the judiciary. He served as Chief Justice of the Sudan (1964-7) after being active in the 1964 Revolution. He resigned as Chief Justice in protest over the issue of banning communists from Parliament. After the 1969 Revolution he was named the first Prime Minister in the new regime. He also served, at various times, as Minister of Foreign Affairs, of Justice, and as Deputy Prime Minister before resigning for reasons of health in 1972.

AWLAD JABIR. "The children of Jabir" were major reli-

gious leaders in the Nilotic Sudan from the 16th until the
mid-18th century.   They, their kinsmen through marriage,
and their descendants formed a complex of holy families
that maintained important schools and provided religious
leadership in the Sudan.   Their ancestry is traced back
traditionally to a wandering 15th-century scholar, Ghulamallah ibn Ayid.   Little is known about Jabir, but his
offspring gained fame: Ibrahim al-Bulad, Abd al-Rahman, and Ismail established major schools in the Shayqiyyah (q. v.) area, while his scholar daughter was the
teacher and mother of the continuing line of scholars in
the family.   Her most famous children were Muhammad
al-Sughayrun, who was granted land by a Funj sultan and
was a political as well as religious force in the sultanate,
and Amina, a learned woman whose sons set up schools
in the Shandi area.

AZANDE.   A large grouping of tribes speaking a language
belonging to the Adamawa-Eastern group (q. v.).   They
began migrating into the southwestern Sudan in the 16th
century.   In the 18th century the Avungara, a military
aristocracy, imposed its control over the Zande groups
and created a series of well-organized kingdoms.   These
kingdoms were the dominant force in the southwestern
Sudan until the 20th century.   Zande leaders like Yambio (q. v.) resisted British rule, while others, like Tambura (q. v.) cooperated.   After World War II an attempt
was made, through the Zande Scheme (q. v.), to aid in
development but this did not have a major impact.

AZANIA LIBERATION FRONT (ALF).   A southern political
organization formed in 1965.   Following the split in
SANU (q. v.), members of SANU-in exile formed the ALF
under Joseph Oduho (q. v.) and Father Saturnino (q. v.).
The Sudan African Liberation Front, formed by Aggrey
Jaden, merged with the ALF late in 1965.   Personal and
tribal rivalries divided the ALF and most of its leadership went to the Southern Sudan Provisional Government
(q. v.) when it was formed in 1967.

AZHARI, al-.   This means "from al-Azhar," the great Islamic university in Cairo.   In the Sudan, "al-Azhari" is
associated most frequently with a branch of the family
of Ismail al-Wali (q. v.).   Ismail's son Ahmad (ca. 1810-
1881) was educated at al-Azhar and was a prominent 19th-
century Sudanese legal scholar.   In contrast to his broth-
er, who was the leader of the Ismailiyyah (q. v.), Ahmad

al-Azhari opposed Mahdism and was killed in an early
battle. Ahmad's son, Ismail al-Azhari (1868-1947), be-
came a judge of Islamic law and served as Mufti of the
Sudan (1924-32). Ismail's grandson, another Ismail al-
Azhari (q.v.), became the first Prime Minister of the
independent Sudan. Other members of the family, like
Ibrahim al-Mufti (q.v.), were also prominent in modern
Sudanese politics.

AZHARI, ISMAIL, al-, 1902-69. The first Prime Minister
of the independent Sudan. He was educated in Gordon
College and the American University of Beirut. He served as a mathematics teacher in the Department of Education (1921-46) and was a major figure in the development of Sudanese nationalism that favored Nile valley
unity. He was a founder and leader of the Graduates
Congress (q.v.), the Ashigga Party (q.v.), and was the
president of the NUP when it was formed in 1952. After the NUP victory in the 1953 elections, al-Azhari became the first Sudanese Prime Minister, a post that he
held at the time of the Sudan's formal gaining of independence. His cabinet fell in 1956 after a split within
the NUP. In the Abboud era he was out of politics but
active in opposition. After the 1964 Revolution he led
the NUP to political importance, usually in alliance with
the Umma Party (q.v.). He was elected the permanent
president of the Supreme Council, serving until the 1969
Revolution. He was a descendant of the 19th-century religious leader, Ismail al-Wali (q.v.), and a grandson of
a Mufti of the Sudan. (See al-AZHARI.)

AZMIYYAH. A muslim group established by Muhammad
Madi Abu al-Aza'im (1870-1936). The founder was an
Egyptian school teacher in the Sudan who was deported
in 1915 because of his political views. He was influenced by Wahhabi (q.v.) teachings and advocated a vigorous reform of Islam and opposition to the influence of
the hereditary religious leaders. Membership in his organization reached a peak in the 1920's.

-B-

"B." Between two proper names, b. stands for ibn, meaning "son of..."

B-GROUP. This is the name given to the Nubian culture

that emerged after the Egyptian conquest of lower Nubia
around 2600 B. C.   It is considered a time of local cultural decadence and some new elements, although scholars disagree on the degree of distinctiveness from A-
Group culture (q. v.).   The B-Group period ends in the
First Intermediate Period of Egyptian history, ca. 2160
B. C.

BADI II, ABU DIQN.   Funj sultan of Sennar, ruling from
1645 until 1681.   His reign marked the peak of the dynasty's power and prosperity.   He defeated potential en-
emies in the White Nile and Nuba Mountain areas, built
the royal palace and first major mosque in Sennar, and
encouraged trade and religious scholarship.   Using slaves
from his conquests he created a corps of slave troops
which later caused tensions with the old Funj aristocracy.

BADRI, BABIKIR, d. 1954.   Sudanese educationist and intellectual.   As a young man he was a soldier in the Mahdist army.   In the 20th-century he became a pioneer in
modern education in a traditional context.   He is called
the "father of girls' education in the Sudan," establishing
the first Sudanese girls' school in 1908.   He and his
family were active in 20th-century intellectual developments in the Sudan.

BAGGARA see BAQQARA

BAHAN CULTURE.   Khor Bahan is the site of the discovery
of the earliest known evidence of Neolithic culture in
Nubia, with a possible date of 3500 B. C.

BAKER PASHA, SIR SAMUEL W. , 1821-1893.   British adventurer and traveler.   After many different ventures
around the world, he came to the Sudan in 1861 to ex-
plore the upper Nile region.   In 1869 the ruler of Egypt
appointed him governor-general of the southern provinces
of the Sudan.   Baker traveled widely in the south trying
to force the tribes to submit to governmental control.
In 1873 he left the Sudan.   He wrote many books on his
activities in the Sudan and elsewhere.

BAKHEIT, JA'FAR MUHAMMAD ALI, d. 1976.   Sudanese
intellectual and political leader.   He was active in political and ideological affairs after the 1969 Revolution.
He was one of the drafters of the permanent constitution, editor of the official newspaper, al-Sahafa, and

at various times, Minister of Local Government, Assistant Secretary-General and Secretary General of the SSU.

BALLANA CULTURE. Recent scholarship sometimes uses this name for the X-Group culture (q. v.) in Nubia of the A. D. 300's-600's.

BAN AL-NAQA see YA'QUBAB

BANAGGA. A form of Ban al-Naqa. See YA'QUBAB.

BAQQARA. A large group of Arab tribes principally found in Darfur and Kordofan. They are primarily cattle-herding peoples with a reputation for being warlike. They gave active support to the Mahdist movement and the Khalifah Abdallahi (q. v.) was from the Ta'ishi tribe of Baqqara. Other major Baqqara tribes are the Rizayqat, Homr, and Messiriyyah.

BARING, EVELYN, 1st Earl of Cromer, 1841-1917. British administrator and financier. After the British occupation of Egypt in 1882, he became the British agent and consul-general there and was the virtual ruler of the country until his retirement in 1907. He dominated the formulation of British policy regarding the Sudan during those years. He was the principal architect of the "Condominium" (q. v.) structure which governed the Sudan from 1899 until 1956.

BEHEIRY, MAMOUN, 1925- . Sudanese banker and economist. He was educated at Oxford University and worked in the Ministry of Finance. He was governor of the Bank of Sudan (1960-64), Minister of Finance (1964), and first President of the African Development Bank (1965-1970). After the Addis Ababa Agreement of 1972 (q. v.) he was named chairman of the Relief and Resettlement Fund for the South and in 1975 became the Minister of Finance.

BEJA. A group of nomadic tribes inhabiting the areas in the Sudan between the Red Sea and the Nile. They are often traced back to the ancient Blemmyes (q. v.). After the A. D. 600's they gradually converted to Islam and the modern tribal units began to emerge by the 16th-century. These units are the Ababda (q. v.), Bishariyyin (q. v.), Amarar (q. v.), Hadandowa (q. v.) and Beni Amir (q. v.). Some tribal sections participated in the wars of

the Mahdiyyah: the Hadandowa and some Amarar joined
the Mahdist forces while other groups were anti-Mahdist,
following Khatmiyyah (q.v.) leadership. In the 20th-cen-
tury the Beja remained aloof from national political developments although in the 1960's there was a Beja political party, the Beja Congress (q.v.).

BEJA CONGRESS. A political organization representing regional and tribal interests of the Beja tribes (q.v.) in
the eastern Sudan. It won 10 seats in the parliamentary
elections of 1965. The Congress remained in existence
until the abolition of political parties in 1969 but had won
only three seats in the elections in 1968.

BEY. A civil and military title below pasha (q.v.) in rank
in the old Ottoman and Egyptian systems.

BISHARIN. A Beja (q.v.) nomadic tribe. According to tradition they moved into part of their present area on the
western slopes of the Red Sea hills in the 15th-century
and moved into the Atbara River area under a great chief,
Hamad Imran, around 1760. There are two major sections, the Umm Ali and the Umm Naji. They were not
very active in the Mahdiyyah or 20th-century national
developments.

BLACK FRONT. A group reported to be working in the
southern Sudan in 1948 among southern government staff.
It advocated no interference by northerners in the south
and demanded "the South for the Southerners."

BLEMMYES. A tribal group on the east bank of the Nile in
the last years of the kingdom of Kush (q.v.). Expanding
their area they came into conflict with the Romans in
Egypt. The Romans attempted to create a buffer state
in Nobatia (q.v.) but the Nobatae later fought beside the
Blemmyes against the Romans. The Blemmyes did not
convert readily to Christianity and were destroyed by
wars with the Kingdom of Dongola in the A.D. 500's.
Some scholars trace the origins of the modern Beja
tribes (q.v.) to the Blemmyes.

-C-

C-GROUP. The local cultural group in lower Nubia from
the 2100's B.C. until around 1520 B.C. It may have

been the product of migrations of new peoples into the
area at the time of an Egyptian withdrawal. However,
some believe C-Group culture to be a development of
the A and B Groups cultures (qq. v.). The C-Group was
contemporary with but distinct from the Kerma culture
(q. v.). It gained a degree of political and cultural independence from Egypt during the Hyksos Period but was crushed
by the revived Egyptian Empire of the New Kingdom.

CENTRAL SUDANIC PEOPLES. A linguistic grouping of
southern Sudanese peoples who speak languages of the
Central Sudanic subfamily of the larger Nilo-Saharan
family. They are scattered in the Bahr al-Ghazal and
Equatoria regions and include the Njangulgule, Shatt, and
Kreish.

COMBONI, DANIELE, 1831-1881. An Italian missionary in
the Roman Catholic Church. He came to the Sudan in
1857 and returned to Italy in 1859. He proposed a program for missions to Africa utilizing an African priesthood. He gained support and recognition and was able
to establish, in 1867, a training center in Verona, Italy.
In 1872 he was appointed pro-vicar apostolic for central
Africa and he returned to the Sudan where he established
missions and schools. After his death the work continued and the "Verona Fathers" were an important force
in missions and education.

COMMUNIST PARTY OF THE SUDAN (CPS). There was
scattered activity by individual Communists in the Sudan
before World War II. In 1946 a formal organization was
created in the Sudan called the Sudan Movement for National Liberation, which was an offshoot of the Egyptian
Communist movement. During the 1940's and 1950's the
CPS operated through various front organizations. It
was especially important among students, forming the
Students Congress (1949) and then the Democratic Front
(1954). It contested elections through the Anti-Imperialist Front (q. v.). The party developed an orthodox, Moscow-oriented wing, led by Abd al-Khaliq Mahjub (q. v.)
and a wing emphasizing local Sudanized Marxism. The
CPS joined in opposition to the Abboud regime and played
an important role in the 1964 Revolution and the subsequent transition government. In the 1960's the CPS openly contested elections but came into conflict with the
Umma-NUP coalition governments. An attempt to outlaw
the CPS created a major constitutional crisis in 1965-7.

In this, some members created a more broadly conceiv-
ed Socialist Party of the Sudan (1967-9), while others advocated operating underground. After the 1969 Revolution
the CPS gained influence. The nationalist wing of the
party, led by Ahmad Sulayman (q.v.) and Faruq Abu Issa
(q.v.), cooperated with the new regime but the Mahjub
faction was less supportive. Mahjub was arrested in 1970
and exiled for a time. The major crisis came in July 1971,
when pro-Communist officers attempted unsuccessfully to
overthrow the government. In the aftermath Mahjub and
other CPS leaders were executed along with the dissident
officers and the party organization was crushed. The
nationalist Marxists have maintained a role in the revolutionary regime and have not created a separate organization.

CONDOMINIUM. The term usually used to describe the governmental structure of the Sudan in 1899-1956. It was
defined in the Anglo-Egyptian Agreement of 1899, with
some later modifications. Although it theoretically provided for some governing role for Egypt, in practice the
structure insured full British control over the Sudan.
The Anglo-Egyptian Agreement of 1953 defined the steps
leading to the end of the Condominium arrangement.

CROMER see BARING, EVELYN

-D-

D-GROUP. The name given by early 20th-century scholars
to sites and remains in Nubia dating after 1500 B.C.,
in the period of Egyptian New Kingdom control of the
region.

DAFTARDAR. A title for an official responsible for maintaining registers, usually financial. In Sudanese history,
"the Daftardar" often means Muhammad Khusraw (q.v.).

DAJU. An early dynasty ruling a small state in Darfur before Islamic times, gaining control sometime before
1200 A.D. and being replaced by the Tunjur (q.v.) sometime between the 14th and 16th centuries.

DANAQLA. Arabized people with many Nubian elements from
the region of Dongola. They have had long interaction
with the Jaaliyyin (q.v.) and have migrated throughout

the Sudan as merchants and traders from at least the
days of the Funj (q.v.).

DARFUR. The western part of the Sudan. The Fur people
(Darfur means "the house of the Fur") are Muslims and
speak a language which is a separate branch of the Nilo-
Saharan language family. Darfur is the region of the
Keira (q.v.) and Tunjur (q.v.) sultanates.

DEMOCRATIC FRONT see COMMUNIST PARTY OF THE
SUDAN

DEMOCRATIC UNIONIST PARTY (DUP). Formed in 1967 as
the result of a merger of the PDP (q.v.) and the NUP
(q.v.). Ismail al-Azhari (q.v.) of the NUP was president and Ali Abd al-Rahman (q.v.) of the PDP was vice-
president. The DUP represented the recreation of the
old alliance between al-Azhari and the Khatmiyyah (q.v.)
that had broken up in 1956. The party came to an official end with the 1969 Revolution.

DENG, FRANCIS. Sudanese scholar and diplomat. He studied law in Khartoum and at Yale University. He taught
at New York University and was a member of the United
Nations Human Rights Commission. He has served in
important diplomatic posts as ambassador to the United
Nations and the United States as well as being, for a
time, Minister of State for Foreign Affairs. He has written many significant anthropological and historical studies, receiving the African Studies Association Herskovits
Prize for one of his books.

DENG, SANTINO, 1922- . Southern administrator and politician from the Dinka tribe. He was educated in Catholic
mission schools and became a government agriculturalist.
He resigned and was elected to Parliament in 1953. He
ran as an independent but joined the NUP (q.v.) and received a cabinet post in 1954. He then accepted a min-
isterial post in the Umma Party (q.v.) government of
1958. He remained as Minister of Animal Resources in
Abboud's cabinet and was the sole southerner in the military regime's government. After the 1964 Revolution he
formed his own party, the Sudan Unity Party, which had
limited influence. The SUP cooperated with northern policies and was opposed by other southern groups.

DENG, WILLIAM. Southern political leader. He started in

the government administrative service and became an
assistant district commissioner. He went into exile
during the Abboud era and was one of the founders, in
1962, of SANU (q.v.). After the 1964 Revolution he returned to the Sudan. In 1965 he claimed to lead the
southern delegation at the Roundtable Conferences. He
broke with the leaders of SANU in exile and was elected
to Parliament in 1967, where he became chairman of the
southern parliamentary group. He was killed while traveling in the south in 1968.

DINKA. The largest group of Nilotes (q.v.) in the Sudan and
the biggest single tribal confederation in the country.
They comprise more than 10 percent of the total Sudanese population and are primarily located in the Bahr al-
Ghazal and White Nile areas. They have been less isolated than most southern tribes and Dinka have taken an
active role in modern politics through men like William
and Francis Deng and Abel Alier. (qq.v.)

DIU, BUTH, 1917-1975. Southern political leader of Nuer
origin. He entered the government service in 1937,
eventually becoming a magistrate. He served in the
Legislative Assembly (q.v.) and on the Constitutional
Commission (1951), and was chairman of Zeraf Island
Rural District Council. He was elected to parliament
in 1953 and formed the Southern Party, which became
the Liberal Party (q.v.) in 1954 with Diu as secretary
general. He served in many cabinets and was elected
to Parliament again in the 1960's. After the 1969 Revolution created the Peoples Assembly in 1973 he was
elected to that body.

DONGOLA, KINGDOM OF. Formed by the union of the earlier Nubian states of Nobatia (q.v.) and Makuria (q.v.)
around A.D. 650-700. It had a long history of relations
with Islamic Egypt. After a successful defense in the
8th-century, the borders were quite stable until a successful Dongolan invasion of upper Egypt in the 10th-cen-
tury. The Dongolans were gradually driven back until
a final defeat at the hands of the Muslims in 1323 brought
an end to the kingdom. The kingdom had been Christian
although in its later years Muslim influences in it grew.

DONGOLAWI (or DUNQULAWI). The singular of Danaqla
(q.v.).

-E-F-

EFENDI or EFFENDI or AFANDE. A general term of address, often equal to "mister. " It also is specifically used to mean an educated person or government official.

EL- . The definite article in Arabic; it is the same as "al- " (q. v.).

FAJR, al-. A leading Sudanese intellectual magazine established in 1934. It brought together many different groups of educated Sudanese and provided a vehicle for the expression of their views. It became more overtly political after the death in 1936 of Arafat Muhammad Abdallah, who had helped to create the journal along with the Hashmab group (q. v.).

FASHODA. A village in the southern Sudan on the White Nile. Its modern name is Kodok. In 1898 a French expedition led by J. B. Marchand occupied Fashoda, laying claim to the upper Nile for France. A major international crisis followed when Anglo-Egyptian forces under H. H. Kitchener (q. v.) forced a French withdrawal. Ultimately French claims were withdrawn and the area became part of the Anglo-Egyptian Sudan in 1899.

FATIMA BINT JABIR see AWLAD JABIR

FEDDAN. A Sudanese unit of area equal to 1. 038 acres.

FEDERAL PARTY. A southern party formed by younger men dissatisfied with the Liberal Party (q. v.) in 1957-8. It was formed by Ezboni Mondiri (q. v.) and advocated a federal form of government. It ceased operation with the 1958 military coup.

FELLATA. A general term applied to West Africans living in the Sudan. It originally referred simply to northern Nigerians. They are Muslims who have come to the Sudan while on pilgrimage to Mecca in Arabia. Many have settled permanently and they are a significant ethnic group in the contemporary Sudan.

FIKI (plural: FUQAHA). The Arabic term for the Muslim religious teacher, usually in rural areas.

FILISTS. The group associated with Shaykh Ahmad al-Sayyid

al-Fil in the Graduates Club during the 1920's and 1930's.
Sayyid Ali al-Mirghani (q.v.) supported the group, which
was in favor of cooperation with Egyptian nationalism and
opposed to the Ansar-backed Shawqists (q.v.).

FREE NEGROES ORGANIZATION see GABOUSH, PHILLIP
ABBAS

FRONT OF PROFESSIONAL ORGANIZATIONS. An alliance
of various groups formed in late 1964 to oppose the Abboud regime. It brought together student, faculty groups
with labor unions, peasant representatives, and professional associations like the Sudan Bar Association. It
played a significant role in the 1964 Revolution and was
a major force in the transition government of 1964-5.
It encouraged a broader role for women in politics and
was closely aligned with the Communist Party. Popular
support for the Front gradually declined as the older
parties were reorganized and as public opinion became
weary and suspicious of the Front's radical pronounce-
ments. By the 1965 elections the Front had basically
broken up into its component parts.

FUNJ SULTANATE. The state controlling much of the Nile
valley in the central Sudan from the beginning of the
16th-century until the Turco-Egyptian invasion in 1820-1.
Funj origins are debated but they may have been a southern Nubian people from the upper White Nile area. The
traditional founder is Amara Dunqas (q.v.) who is said
to have established the capital at Sennar around 1504.
The state was a loosely organized unit with important
sub-kings, including the Abdallab (q.v.). Funj political
culture mixed a growing Islamic influence with pre-Islamic practices and the Funj era was a time of increasing Islamization of northern Sudanese society. The Funj
sultans reached a peak of power under Badi II Abu Duqn
(1644-1681) (q.v.) and then faced growing loss of control
over vassel princes. The line of direct descent from
Amara was broken in 1718 when Funj nobility deposed
Sultan Unsa III. The sultans lost final control of the
state in 1762 when a powerful commander, Muhammad
Abu Likaylik (q.v.), became the real ruler and kingmaker. From then until 1821 his clan, the Hamaj (q.v.),
ruled through puppet sultans. The final years of the
sultanate were filled with revolts and civil wars which
opened the way for the Turco-Egyptian conquest.

FUR see DARFUR

FUZZY-WUZZY. A name popularized by Rudyard Kipling,
    refering to the Beja (q.v.) tribesmen of the eastern Su-
    dan. Their fighting ability during the Mahdiyyah inspired
    Kipling, especially when they "broke the British square"
    at the Battle of Tamai in 1884.

-G-

GABOUSH, PHILLIP ABBAS. Nuba politician and revolution-
    ary. He was a leader in the General Union of Nubas
    (q.v.) and was elected to Parliament in 1965. He advo-
    cated regional autonomy for non-Arabs in the northern
    Sudan and organized the secret Free Negroes Organiza-
    tion in 1967. He then created the United Front for the
    Liberation of the African Sudan in 1969 and planned a
    coup which was preempted by the 1969 Revolution. His
    concept of "Black Power" and non-Arab autonomy in the
    north received little public support and was ignored by
    southern activists.

GARANG, ENOCH MADENG DE. Southern journalist and po-
    litical leader. He was a theology student and Presby-
    terian church official. He became the director of the
    London-based Southern Sudan Association (q.v.) and ed-
    ited its journal, Grass Curtain. He had ties with the
    South Sudan Liberation Movement (q.v.) and was a mem-
    ber of the southern delegation at the Addis Ababa talks.
    Since the 1972 settlement he has held a number of posts
    in the Southern Region High Executive Committee.

GARANG, JOSEPH, d. 1971. Southern lawyer and political
    leader. He was an active member of the Communist
    Party and held important cabinet posts, especially Min-
    ister for Southern Affairs (1969-1971) in the government
    after the 1969 Revolution. He was executed in July 1971
    for complicity in the leftist attempt to overthrow the
    Numayri regime.

GENERAL UNION OF NUBAS. An organization representing
    Nuba (q.v.) tribal and regional interests. It contested
    elections and won a few parliamentary seats in the 1960's,
    when it was led by Phillip Abbas Gaboush (q.v.).

GEZIRA SCHEME. A major agricultural project in the Ge-

zira area. It was planned before World War I but only
went into full operation in the 1920's. It was originally
a joint venture between a private company (the Sudan
Plantations Syndicate), the Sudan Government, and the
local farmers. Its cotton production became a mainstay
of the Sudanese economy. After independence the role
of the private company was taken over by the government.
The area within the Scheme has been extended a number
of times and the Gezira Scheme has been used as a mod-
el by other African governments impressed by its success.

GEZIRA TENANTS UNION. This association was created in
1953 when the representative council for tenants in the
Gezira Scheme (q. v.) was recognized as a trade union.
The tenants had engaged in organized action in support
of their interests previously. The Union was one of the
largest and best organized economic interest groups in
the Sudan. It became involved in national politics, usually in alliance with the more radical parties. Its president was al-Amin Muhammad al-Amin, a communist political activist. He was in the cabinet from time to time
and led the Union to an important role in the 1964 Revolution. In the changed political situation after the 1969
Revolution, the organization of the Union was changed,
although the tenants remain active.

GHULAMALLAH IBN 'AYID see AWLAD JABIR

GORDON, CHARLES, 1833-1885. British soldier and adventurer. After military service in a number of different
parts of the world, he came to the Sudan as an administrator in the Turco-Egyptian regime, ultimately serving
as governor-general (1877-80). He left the Sudan briefly
and then returned in 1884 with the task of completing the
Egyptian evacuation of the country in the face of the Mahdist advances. He was killed in 1885 when the Mahdist
forces captured Khartoum. His dynamic personality and
career captured the imagination of the British public and
he has been the subject of a large and often romanticiz-
ing body of literature.

GORDON COLLEGE OLD BOYS CLUB see GRADUATES
CLUB

GORDON MEMORIAL COLLEGE. An educational institution
in Khartoum. It was established with the support of a

large public subscription in Britain in memory of Charles
Gordon (q. v.). The school was opened in 1902 and was
an important part of the educational system, being both
a major training center for the government services and
also the breeding ground for the class of educated Sudanese nationalists. The college program developed and it
became the core of the University College of Khartoum
which was created in 1951 and later became the University of Khartoum.

GRADUATES CLUB. The "Old Boys" Club for Gordon Memorial College, formed in 1918. It provided a forum for
discussion among the educated Sudanese and was a focus
for early factional disputes, especially between the Filists
(q. v.) and the Shawqiats (q. v.). Its political functions
passed to the Graduates Congress (q. v.).

GRADUATES CONGRESS. The early nationalist organization
in the Sudan. It was formed in 1938 by people from all
the different groups among the educated classes in the
Sudan. Early leaders included Ismail al-Azhari (q. v.),
Muhammad Ahmad Mahjub (q. v.), and Ahmad Khayr
(q. v.). It hoped for independence but soon split into
more militant nationalists supporting Nile valley unity
and those supporting a separate, independent Sudan. The
British rejection of a Congress memorandum asking for
self-rule in 1942 hastened an open split between the two
factions. By the end of World War II the Congress organization was under the control of the supporters of
Nile valley unity. In the postwar era, the Congress was
just one of many Sudanese political organizations. It
became a part of the NUP (q. v.) in 1952 and the Congress was formally dissolved.

GRASS CURTAIN see SOUTHERN SUDAN ASSOCIATION

-H-

HAMAD, AHMAD AL-SAYYID. Sudanese lawyer and political
leader. He was secretary-general of the PDP and then
the DUP (after 1967). He held many cabinet positions:
Minister of Irrigation (1964-5), of Commerce (1967-8),
Communications (1968). He was identified with Khatmiyyah (q. v.) political interests in the days of party politics.
After the 1969 Revolution he was tried and convicted of
corruption by the Peoples Court of the Revolutionary Government.

HAMAD, HAMAD TAWFIQ, 1904- . Sudanese businessman
and political leader. He was educated in Gordon College
and joined the Finance Department in 1924. He later became the first Sudanese to hold the rank of Inspector of
Accounts for the Department of Agriculture. He left government service in 1947 to pursue his business, farming,
and political interests. He was one of the founders of
the Graduates Congress (q. v.) and was secretary of the
National Front Party (q. v.) until that party joined the
NUP. He became a member of the NUP executive committee and was elected to Parliament in 1953. He resigned from the NUP in 1956 and helped to create the
PDP (q. v.) of which he became director-general. He
served as a cabinet minister both with the NUP and the
PDP, acting as Minister of Finance (1954-6), of Communications (1956), and of Commerce and Industry (1956-8).
After the Abboud regime came to power, Hamad became
managing director and then chairman of the Agricultural
Bank of the Sudan, continuing in that post in the 1960's.

HAMAD, KHIDR, 1910- . Sudanese political leader. He
was a graduate of Gordon Memorial College and worked
in the Finance Department. He was a member of the
Abu Ra'uf group (q. v.) of intellectuals in the 1930's. In
1946 he joined the Finance Department of the Arab League
and then returned to enter politics. He was a member
of the Ashigga (q. v.) and became secretary-general of
the NUP (q. v.) in 1952. He was elected to Parliament
(1953-8) and served in Ismail al-Azhari's (q. v.) cabinet.
After the 1964 Revolution he was made a member of the
Supreme Council and was reelected to Parliament in 1968.
He was not active publically after the 1969 Revolution.

HAMAD AL-MAJDHUB see MAJDHUBIYYAH

HAMADALLAH, FARUQ UTHMAN, d. 1971. Sudanese soldier
and political leader. He had been prematurely retired
before the 1969 Revolution and was restored to active
rank by the Council of the Revolution, of which he was
a member. He served in the key post of Minister of
Interior until he was dismissed from his civil and military positions in November, 1970. He was one of the
leaders of the attempted revolution in July, 1971, and
was executed after that movement's failure.

HAMAJ. A pre-Arab, pre-Funj grouping in the Blue Nile
region south of Sennar. They rose to politico-military
importance in the Funj Sultanate (q. v.) during the 18th-

century under the leadership of Muhammad Abu Likaylik
(q. v.). He and his clan became kingmakers after 1761,
ruling through puppet kings while assuming the simple
title of wazir, or secretary. The Hamaj were unable to
prevent the disintegration of the sultanate in a series of
civil wars. The last Hamaj "regent" was executed during the Turco-Egyptian conquest of 1821.

HAMZA, MIRGHANI, 1897- . Sudanese engineer and political leader of Danaqla origin. He was educated in Gordon
Memorial College and entered the Public Works Department. He served in a wide variety of posts, eventually
becoming the first Sudanese to gain the rank of Assistant
Director of Works (1948-53). He was active in a wide
variety of political organizations, being one of the founders of the Graduates Congress (q. v.) and serving on the
Advisory Council for the Northern Sudan (q. v.). He was
associated with Khatmiyyah (q. v.) political interests and
refused the post of Minister of Works in the Legislative
Assembly (q. v.). He was on the Constitutional Commission later. He helped to organize the NUP and served
on its executive committee. He was in the cabinet of
Ismail al-Azhari (q. v.) but broke with him and formed
the Independent Republican Party (q. v.) which was dissolved when the Khatmiyyah-supported PDP was created
in 1956.

HARKHUF. An Egyptian governor in Aswan who made four
trips for exploration and trade into Nubia and the Sudan
around the 22nd-century B. C. Reports from his trips
are important sources for early Sudanese history.

HASHMAB GROUP. A literary and nationalist discussion
group in the 1920's and 1930's composed of younger graduates. In 1934 the group organized the publication of
al-Fajr, a magazine emphasizing the intellectual rather
than the more narrowly political aspects of nationalism.
Muhammad Ahmad Mahjub (q. v.) was among the organizers of the group.

HINDI, ABD AL-RAHMAN, al-, d. 1964. The son of Yusuf
al-Hindi (q. v.) and his successor as leader of the Hindiyyah order. He had local influence in the Blue Nile area
but was not as prominent as his father. As Sudan gained independence, he formed the short-lived National Party
which soon merged with the NUP (q. v.).

HINDI, HUSAYN SHARIF YUSUF, al-, ca. 1925- . Sudanese
  religious leader and politician. He was a son of Yusuf
  al-Hindi (q.v.) who entered politics after the 1964 Revolution. He was a member of the NUP (q.v.) and held
  many cabinet posts: Minister of Irrigation (1965-6), of
  Finance (1966 and 1967-8), of local government (1966-7).
  After the 1969 Revolution he was said to be a leading
  organizer of movements against the revolutionary regime.

HINDI, SHARIF YUSUF, al- see HINDI, YUSUF IBN
  MUHAMMAD AL-AMIN, al-

HINDI, YUSUF IBN MUHAMMAD AL-AMIN, al-, ca. 1865-
  1942. A religious leader whose followers form the Hindiyyah order, an offshoot of the Sammaniyyah (q.v.). The
  family is recognized as being among the ashraf or descendants of the Prophet Muhammad. Yusuf fought on
  the side of the Mahdists as a young man but after the
  Anglo-Egyptian conquest he assisted the new regime. He
  gained numerous followers as a religious leader and had
  substantial informal political influence. He was a member of the Sudanese delegation that went to London in
  1919 to congratulate the king on Britain's victory in World
  War I. His advice and support was sought in the early
  days of the Sudanese nationalist movement but he died
  before the days of formal party politics. His son and
  khalifah (q.v.) was Abd al-Rahman al-Hindi (q.v.).

HINDIYYAH see HINDI, YUSUF IBN MUHAMMAD AL-
  AMIN, al-

HUSAYN AL-KHALIFAH MUHAMMAD SHARIF, 1888-1928.
  A pioneer in Sudanese journalism. He was a grandson
  of the Mahdi and graduated from Gordon Memorial College (1912). He was editor of the important early Arabic newspapers, al-Ra'id al-Sudan (1917-9) and al-Hadarat
  al-Sudan (1920-8). His work set the style and tone for
  much of early Sudanese journalism.

                              -I-

IBN. Between two proper names or preceding a proper name,
  ibn means "son of..."

IBRAHIM, ABU AL-QASIM MUHAMMAD. Sudanese soldier

and political leader. He was a member of the original
Council of the Revolution in 1969 and served in a wide
range of cabinet and government positions. His cabinet
posts include Minister of Local Government (1969-71),
of Interior (1970-1), of Health (1971-4), of Agriculture
(1974 into 1976). He also served at times as Assistant
Premier for Services and Local Government (1970-1) and
in the SSU Political Bureau.

IBRAHIM, FATMA AHMAD. Sudanese journalist and femin-
ist. She was the publisher of Sawt al-Mar'a, a women's
journal suspended by the government in 1966. She was
active in the Communist Party and was the president of
the Sudanese Women's Federation which was dissolved
by the government in 1971. She was reported to have
been jailed in 1976.

IBRAHIM AL-BULAD see AWLAD JABIR

IDRIS IBN ARBAB, 1507-1650. A religious teacher of great
fame during the Funj (q.v.) era who, according to tradition, lived 147 lunar years. He was respected and
consulted by the Funj nobility and served as a mediator
in major political disputes. He was a leader of the Qadiriyyah (q.v.) and his tomb at Aylafun became an important religious center.

IDRISIYYAH. The tariqah (q.v.) led by the descendants of
Ahmad ibn Idris (q.v.). At first his sons were association with his prominent students' tariqahs, especially
the Sanusiyyah (q.v.) and the Rashidiyyah (q.v.). Then
Abd al-Muta'al ibn Ahmad (1790-1878) came to the Sudan
and established the influence of the family and order in
the Dongola area. Members of the family settled in upper Egypt and in the Asir in the Arabian Peninsula.
There Muhammad ibn Ali (1876-1923) created an independent state during World War I and was finally absorbed into Saudi Arabia in 1930. The branches of the family maintained close contacts but in the Sudan, as elsewhere, it had a declining influence. It often clashed
with the Mirghani family (q.v.).

IMAM. A Muslim religious leader, especially a leader in
prayer. In the Sudan, the leader of the Ansar (q.v.)
organization in the 20th-century was called "the Imam."

INDEPENDENCE FRONT (al-Jibhat al-Istiqlaliyyah). A co-

alition of parties favoring an independent Sudan formed
in 1945, primarily for purposes of political discussions
in Cairo. The parties involved were the Umma (q. v.),
Republican (q. v.), the Nationalist Party (q. v.), and the
Liberal Party (q. v.).

INDEPENDENT REPUBLICAN PARTY. A party formed in
    1954 by three leaders of the NUP (q. v.) who were pro-
    Khatmiyyah: Mirghani Hamza (q. v.), Khalafalla Khalid,
    and Ahmad Geili. The first two had been ministers in
    Ismail al-Azhari's (q. v.) cabinet but had been dismissed
    late in 1954. With the support of Ali al-Mirghani (q. v.),
    the three formed the Independent Republican Party, ad-
    vocating an independent Sudanese republic which would
    cooperate with Egypt. The party was dissolved when
    the Khatmiyyah-supported PDP (q. v.) was created in
    1956.

IRTET. An independent Nubia kingdom in the 3rd millen-
    ium B. C.

ISLAMIC CHARTER FRONT see MUSLIM BROTHERHOOD

ISLAMIC MOVEMENT FOR LIBERATION see MUSLIM
    BROTHERHOOD

ISMAIL AL-WALI, 1793-1863. A religious leader in Kordo-
    fan and the founder of the Ismailiyyah Tariqah (q. v.).
    He was a descendant of a religious teacher in Funj times,
    Bishara al-Gharbawi, and his father was a merchant who
    had settled in Kordofan. Ismail was a student of Mu-
    hammad Uthman al-Mirghani, founder of the Khatmiyyah
    (q. v.) but he attained sufficient prestige to be enabled to
    establish his own religious brotherhood. Ismail's descen-
    dants were active in both religious and political develop-
    ments in the modern Sudan and include Ismail al-Azhari
    (q. v.).

ISMAIL KAMIL PASHA, 1795-1822. The third son of Mu-
    hammad Ali (q. v.), the Ottoman governor of Egypt. He
    commanded the Turco-Egyptian armies that conquered the
    Sudan in 1820-2. He was killed by Nimr (q. v.), a Su-
    danese tribal leader in Shandi. His murder sparked an
    unsuccessful revolt against the newly established Turco-
    Egyptian rule.

ISMAILIYYAH TARIQAH. A tariqah (q. v.) established by

Ismail al-Wali (q.v.) in the 19th-century. In origin it
is related to the Khatmiyyah (q.v.) but it is an independent brotherhood. The leadership of the order passed to
a son of Ismail, Muhammad al-Makki (died 1906), who
became an active supporter of the Mahdist movement.
Another son, Ahmad al-Azhari (see al-AZHARI) opposed
Mahdism, as did his descendants. After 1906 there was
some tension among the family leaders over the leadership of the order. However, the order continued to be
active, with most of its followers concentrated in Kordofan.

-J-

JAALIYIN. One of the two large groupings of Arab tribes
in the Sudan based on traditional genealogies. The Jaaliyin grouping includes a wide variety of tribes claiming
noble descent from the tribe of the Prophet Muhammad.
In general they are settled rather than nomadic tribes
and in composition show continuity with the pre-Arab
population. The core area is the Nile valley from southern Nubia to the Gezira area, although many groups have
migrated into central and western areas.
    Many non-Arab tribes maintain traditional stories of
the intermarriage of their leading families with Jaaliyin
travelers. For the past two centuries merchants operating outside the river valley, called Jallaba (q.v.), were
frequently of Jaaliyin or Danaqla (q.v.) origin. In a
more limited sense, Jaaliyin refers to tribes dominating
the Nile valley between the Atbara River and the Sabaluka
Cataract. Their chiefs or makks (q.v.) were important
leaders in the Funj (q.v.) era and their capital at Shendi
was a religious and commercial center of some importance. Nimr (q.v.) led an early revolt against Turco-
Egyptian rule in 1822. Jaaliyin merchants prospered in
the 19th-century but many supported the Mahdi. They
lost influence in the Mahdist movement during the time
of the Khalifah Abdallahi (q.v.). In the 20th-century
they prospered under the conditions of modernization and
have had an important role in national politics.

JABIR, SONS OF see AWLAD JABIR

JADEN, AGGREY. Southern political leader. He went into
exile during the Abboud era and was a founder of SANU
(q.v.). He was a SANU spokesman at the Roundtable in

Khartoum in 1965 but then returned to exile where he was
active in the Sudan African Liberation Front (q.v.), then
the ALF (q.v.), and then the Southern Sudan Provisional
Government (q.v.).

JALLABA. Small scale merchants and traders operating
throughout the Sudan. Primarily the term applies to
Arab merchants from the riverain groups like the Jaaliyin (q.v.) and Danaqla (q.v.) who operated in non-Arab
areas in the western and southern parts of the Sudan.

JONGLEI SCHEME. A major development scheme along the
White Nile. It involves a canal to keep the water from
being lost in the swamp or sudd (q.v.) regions and an
extensive agricultural scheme.

JUHAYNA. One of the two large groupings of Arab tribes
in the Sudan based on traditional genealogies. The original Juhayna is a tribe in the Arabian Peninsula, sections of which have migrated to Africa from time to
time over the past 1300 years. In the Sudan, "Juhayna"
tribes tended to maintain nomadic lifestyles. Major
tribes in this grouping are the Kababish (q.v.), Baqqara
(q.v.), and Shukriyyah (q.v.). "Juhayna" also has a
more restricted meaning, referring to a nomadic tribe in
the Sennar area.

JULIAN. A Monophysite Christian missionary who was sent
by the Empress Theodora to Nubia in competition with
Orthodox missionaries sent by Justinian. In A.D. 543
he succeeded in converting the rulers of Nobatia (q.v.).

-K-

KABABISH. A great Arab tribe in the northern Sudan of the
Juhayna (q.v.) group. They are concentrated in Kordofan and are a major camel-herding tribe. They suffered
under the Mahdiyyah and their head shaykh was executed
by the Mahdi in 1883. However, the tribal organization
survived and in the 20th-century their leaders were among
the most powerful tribal notables in the country. Ali
al-Tom (q.v.) was influential during the British rule and
members of the family still hold positions of some political importance. In the days of the political parties the
Kababish, being neither Ansar (q.v.) nor Khatmiyyah
(q.v.), generally supported the NUP (q.v.).

KASHTA. A ruler of Kush (q.v.) who began the conquest of Egypt, thus setting the stage for the Kushite 25th Dynasty in Egypt. He was succeeded in 751 B.C. by his son Piankhi (q.v.).

KEIRA SULTANATE. The ruling local dynasty in Darfur from about 1640 until 1916. The Keira were the chiefly clan in the Kunjara branch of the Fur. Power in Darfur passed from the Tunjur (q.v.) to the Keira in a now obscure manner associated with the legendary figure of a "Wise Stranger," Ahmad al- Ma'qur (q.v.). Sulayman Solong (q.v.) was the first historical Keira sultan. These sultans presided over the gradual Islamization of Darfur and had a wide range of contacts with the rest of the Islamic world. The Sultanate was threatened by the Turco-Egyptian conquest of the riverain Sudan in 1821 but Turco-Egyptian control did not extend to Darfur until the defeat of Sultan Ibrahim in 1874 by Zubayr Pasha Rahma (q.v.). Claimants to the throne struggled against Egyptian and then Mahdist control but did not succeed until Ali Dinar (q.v.) secured autonomy in the British controlled Sudan after 1898. In 1916 Ali Dinar answered the Ottoman sultan's call to holy war and revolted against the British. He was quickly defeated and the Keira sultanate came to an end.

KERMA CULTURE. A thriving Sudanese culture centered around Kerma, contemporary with but distinct from the C-Group (q.v.). It flourished at the time of the Middle Kingdom and Second Intermediate Period in Egypt, having good relations with the Hyksos invaders of Egypt. It was crushed by the Egyptian conquest of Nubia in 1530-1520 B.C.

KHALID, MANSUR, 1931- . Sudanese lawyer and diplomat. He studied at the universities of Khartoum, Pennsylvania, Algiers, and Paris. After practicing as a lawyer in Khartoum, he worked in the United Nations Secretariat (1961-2), in Algiers with UN Technical Assistance (1963-4) and in Paris with UNESCO (1965-9). After the 1969 Revolution he was active in governmental affairs, especially in foreign policy. He served as Minister of Youth and Sports (1969-70), at the United Nations as a Sudanese delegate, and then as Foreign Minister (1971-5), and most recently as Minister of Education (1975 into 1976). He played an important role in the negotiations leading up to the Addis Ababa Agreement of 1972 (q.v.).

KHALIFAH. Arabic word meaning "successor" or "deputy. "
It is the title, in tariqahs (q. v.) for the delegate or
spiritual heir of the founder or leader of the brotherhood. As a political title it refers to the Successor to
the Prophet Muhammad in leadership of the Islamic community. (Its common Anglicized form is "caliph. ") In
this usage, Muhammad Ahmad al-Mahdi (q. v.) in the
Sudan gave the title of "khalifah" to his political heirs.
In Sudanese history, reference to "The Khalifah" usually
means Abdallah al-Ta'ishi (q. v.), the Khalifah of the
Mahdi.

KHALIFAH, SIRR AL-KHATIM, al-, 1917- . Sudanese educator and political leader. He was educated in Gordon
Memorial College and joined the Ministry of Education in
1938. He taught and served in a number of educational
administrative posts, including head of the Khartoum
Technical Institute (1960-4) and Deputy Under-Secretary
of the Ministry of Education. After the 1964 Revolution
he was named Prime Minister of the transitional government, serving until June, 1965. He then was made Ambassador to Italy (1965-8) and to Great Britain (1968-9).
After the 1969 Revolution he was retired as Ambassador
to Britain but later was made Minister of Higher Education (1972-3) and then Minister of Education (1973-5).

KHALIL, ABDALLAH, 1888- . Sudanese soldier and politician of Kanza origin. He served in the Egyptian Army
(1910-24) and the Sudan Defence Force (1915-44). He
was the first Sudanese to reach the rank of Miralai (Brig-
adier). He was a founder and the first secretary general of the Umma Party (q. v.) in 1945. He served as
leader of the Legislative Assembly (q. v.) starting in
1948, and was the Umma representative on the Constitutional Commission. He was elected to Parliament in
1953 and became Prime Minister in the Umma-PDP coalition government that replaced Ismail al-Azhari's (q. v.)
government in 1956. He was Prime Minister and Minister of Defense until the military coup by Ibrahim Abboud
(q. v.) in 1958. Some Sudanese believe that Khalil may
have known of and sympathized with Abboud's plans.

KHARTOUM MESOLITHIC. Hunting and gathering culture in
sites near modern Khartoum. It possessed distinctive
pottery, among the oldest known in Africa. Dating is
difficult but there is some evidence for dates around
4000 B. C.

KHARTOUM NEOLITHIC see SHAHEINAB

KHASHM AL-GIRBAH.   An agricultural project and resettlement area in the eastern Sudan near Kassala for people
from Nubia displaced by inundation caused by the building
of the High Dam at Aswan.

KHATMIYYAH.   A tariqah (q.v.) established and led by the
Mirghani family (q.v.).   The founder was Muhammad
Uthman al-Mirghani (1792-1853), a student of Ahmad ibn
Idris (q.v.).   The order was introduced into the Sudan
by Muhammad Uthman during a trip at the end of the
Funj era.   It was firmly established there by his son,
Hasan (1819-1869).   The order developed branches in
Arabia, Egypt, and Eritrea, but its major influence has
been in the Sudan where its history is tied to the exper-
ience of the Mirghani family.   The order is sometimes
called the Mirghaniyyah.   The order is strongest in the
northern and eastern sections of the Sudan.

KHEIR, AHMAD.   Sudanese lawyer and political leader.   He
was educated in Gordon Memorial College and the Khartoum School of Law.   He was active in early intellectual
and nationalist discussion groups.   As a leader of the
Wad Madani Literary Society, he was credited with the
idea for the Graduates Congress (q.v.) and was later active in its work.   He assisted in the writing of the Congress' memorandum in 1942 that set modern Sudanese
politics in motion.   He favored the idea of unity with
Egypt but remained relatively independent of political
parties, although he joined the Ashigga (q.v.) in 1950.
He served as Foreign Minister throughout the Abboud
military period (1958-64) and did not take an active political role after the 1964 Revolution.

KITCHENER, HORATIO HERBERT, 1850-1916.   British soldier and administrator.   After service in the British
Army, he was attached to the Egyptian Army in 1882 and
served in a variety of campaigns in the Sudan during the
Mahdist era.   He was appointed sirdar or commander
of the Egyptian Army in 1892 and led the Anglo-Egyptian
"reconquest" of the Sudan.   He served briefly, in 1899,
as governor-general of the Sudan before taking military
appointments elsewhere in the British Empire.   In 1911-
4 he served as British agent and consul-general in Egypt
and took an active role in laying the foundations for the
future Gezira Scheme (q.v.) in the Sudan.   He was drown-

ed at sea during World War I while serving as British
Secretary of State for War.

KUSH.   This is a name given to the region south of Egyptian
control during the Old and Middle Kingdoms, with some
specific reference to the Kerma Culture (q. v.). After
the Egyptian conquest in 1530 B. C. , Kush was also used
as the term for the Egyptian-controlled area, with the
Egyptian viceroy being known as the "King's Son of Kush. "
With the growing weakness of Egypt in Late Dynastic
times, an independent kingdom of Kush with its capital
at Napata (q. v.) emerged by 860 B. C.   Strong kings of
Napata, e. g. , Piankhi (q. v.), conquered Egypt and formed the 25th Dynasty from around 750 B. C. until defeat
by the Assyrians drove them back to Nubia in ca. 656 B. C.
Kush remained an independent preserver of Egyptian tradition, especially of the Amon-centered religion, for some
time.
    The capital of Kush was moved south to Meroe follow-
ing the destruction of Napata by Psammetichus II during
his invasion from Egypt in 591 B. C.   The Meroe-center-
ed state developed its own distinctive cultural and technological traits although it was strongly influenced by
Hellenistic and Roman as well as ancient Egyptian ideas.
Some scholars see Meroe as a link transmitting Iron Age
technology and other ideas from the Mediterranean and
Near East to sub-Saharan Africa.   Kush faced increasing
pressures and economic decline and its end is usually
said to have come with an invasion from Axum to the
south in A. D. 350.   It was followed by the X-Group culture (q. v.).

-L-

LAGU, JOSEPH.   Southern soldier and political leader. He
was educated in the Sudan Military College and commis-
sioned in the Sudanese Army in 1960.   In 1963 he left
the army and became involved in southern military activities.   By 1968 he was in command of the Anya Nya
(q. v.) forces in eastern Equatoria.   In 1971 he formed
the South Sudan Liberation Movement and he succeeded
in bringing together a wide range of southern guerrilla
and political leaders.   He was the major southern leader
involved in the negotiations leading up to the Addis Ababa
Agreement of 1972 (q. v.) and was able to secure the participation of the southern military forces in the ceasefire

involved in that settlement. He became Inspector-General of the Sudanese Armed Forces and then, in 1974, assumed the post of Officer Commanding, Sudanese Armed Forces in the Southern Region.

LEGISLATIVE ASSEMBLY. An elected, representative assembly created after World War II as a part of the process leading up to Sudanese self-determination. It succeeded the Advisory Council for the Northern Sudan (q. v.) and met certain objections to that body since it contained southern as well as northern representatives and was more fully elective. It was created by an Ordinance in 1948 and had limited powers. Khatmiyyah (q. v.) leaders and the pro-unity of the Nile valley politicians and parties boycotted the Assembly, which meant that it was dominated by Ansar (q. v.) and Umma Party (q. v.) leaders. The leader of the Assembly was Abdallah Khalil (q. v.). The Assembly was replaced by the self-governing parliament elected in 1953 following the Anglo-Egyptian Agreement of 1953.

LIBERAL PARTY (Hizb al-Ahrar). A smaller northern party, formed in 1944. It split in 1945 with the group supporting an independent Sudan joining the Independence Front (q. v.) and gradually being absorbed into the Umma Party (q. v.). Those advocating unity with Egypt, the Liberal Unionists, advocated a federal type system and remained separate until joining in the formation of the NUP (q. v.) in 1952. Among the early Liberal Unionist leaders was Hasan Tahir Zarruq (q. v.).

LIBERAL PARTY (SOUTHERN). Successor to the Southern Party (q. v.) and was formed in 1954 with Buth Diu (q. v.) as Secretary General. The party tended to work with the Umma Party (q. v.) and supported a federal system for the Sudan. The party split into wings led by Stanislaus Paysama (q. v.) and Benjamin Lwoki (q. v.) in 1958. After the 1964 Revolution Paysama was president of a new Liberal Party which contested elections but did not win many parliamentary seats.

LIBERAL UNIONIST PARTY see LIBERAL PARTY (Hizb al-Ahrar)

LOGALI, HILARY PAUL. Sudanese administrator and political leader of Bari origin. He was educated in the University of Khartoum and Yale University, being recalled

from Yale after the 1964 Revolution to become Minister
of Public Works. He was subsequently Minister of Communications (1965) and of Labor (1967-8). He was secretary general and later Vice President of the Southern
Front (q.v.), and was elected to Parliament in 1968.
After the 1969 Revolution he was detained briefly and
was then named Commissioner for Equatoria Province.
After the 1972 settlement he served in the Southern Region High Executive Committee, the Regional Peoples
Assembly and the Sudan Socialist Union (q.v.).

LONGINUS. The successor to Julian (q.v.) as Monophysite
missionary in Nubia. He arrived in Nubia around A.D.
569 and had missionary success in the kingdom of Alwa
(q.v.).

LUO. A variety of groups of Nilotes (q.v.) scattered throughout the southern Sudan, with close ties to tribes in Uganda and Kenya.

LWOKI, BENJAMIN, 1918- . Southern educator and political leader. He served as a school teacher in a number
of schools (1938-48), becoming eventually the first Sudanese headmaster of the Church Missionary Society Primary School in Yei. He was on the boards of the University College of Khartoum and Mundiri Teacher Training College after 1950. He served on the Equatoria Provincial Council and was elected to the Legislative Assembly (q.v.). He was a founder of the Southern Party (q.v.)
and became president of the Liberal Party (q.v.). He
contested leadership with Stanislaus Paysama (q.v.) in
that party. He served in Parliament from 1954-1958.

-M-

MacMICHAEL, HAROLD A., 1883-1969. British administrator. He served in the Sudan Civil Service (1905-33),
acting as Civil Secretary (1926-33) during the important
transition to indirect rule emphasizing local and tribal
administration. He was the author of many important
books and articles on Sudanese history and anthropology.
After leaving the Sudan he served as British High Commissioner for Palestine and Transjordan (1938-44).

MADUOT, TOBY, 1939- . Sudanese doctor and southern
political leader. He took his medical degree in Prague

and had a private practice in Khartoum. He was elected
to Parliament for a Bahr al-Ghazal district in 1968. He
was an active member of the Khartoum-based SANU,
working closely with his brother-in-law, William Deng
(q. v.). After the 1969 Revolution he served in the cabinet and then was named Commissioner for Bahr al-Ghazal Province (1971). After the Addis Ababa Agreement
of 1972 he became a member of the Southern Region
High Executive Council and was elected to the Regional
Peoples Assembly.

MAHDI, al-. In Islamic eschatology, the Mahdi is the di-
vinely-guided leader who would, according to tradition,
"fill the world with justice, even as it has been filled
with injustice," In popular Islam, the idea of the Mahdi
is often associated with messianic expectations. In Sudanese history, "the Mahdi" is most commonly a reference to Muhammad Ahmad al-Mahdi (q. v.).

MAHDI, ABD AL-RAHMAN, al-, 1885-1959. Posthumous son
of Muhammad Ahmad al-Mahdi (q. v.) and leader of the
Ansar. After the defeat of the Mahdist state he was sus-
pected by the British. However, he expressed his firm
support for Britain in World War I and was seen as a
possible counterweight to the influence of Egyptian nationalism in the Sudan. He became very wealthy through
agricultural schemes and organized the Ansar (q. v.) into
an effective political force. He supported a separate,
independent Sudan and his rivalry with Ali al-Mirghani
(q. v.) was a main theme in Sudanese politics. He was
patron of the Umma Party (q. v.) and was a powerful
force in Sudanese politics until his death. (See al-MAH-
DI FAMILY).

MAHDI, MUHAMMAD AHMAD, al-, 1848-1885. A major religious leader and the founder of the Mahdist movement
in the Sudan. He was born in the Dongola area and received a relatively thorough religious education. He became a pupil of Muhammad Sharif Nur al-Da'im (q. v.)
and was initiated into the Sammaniyyah Tariqah (q. v.).
His vigorous asceticism brought him into conflict with
his teacher. He became a strong critic of what he believed was the prevailing immorality of the social and
political leaders of his day. His own zeal and the general popular expectations combined to create the convic-
tion that he was the anticipated Mahdi (q. v.). His support grew rapidly and government attempts to stop the

movement militarily failed. By January 1885 the Mahdi's
forces had taken Khartoum and most of the northern Sudan was under his control. He tried to create an organization modeled on the early Islamic community. Muhammad Ahmad died in Omdurman not long after the conquest
of Khartoum and was succeeded by the Khalifah Abdallahi
al-Ta'ishi (q.v.). The descendants of the Mahdi have
played an important role in 20th-century Sudanese history. (See al-MAHDI FAMILY.)

MAHDI, SADIQ, al-, 1936- . Political and religious leader.
He was a son of Siddiq al-Mahdi and a grandson of Abd
al-Rahman (q.v.). He was educated in Khartoum and
Oxford and served in the Sudanese Parliament. After
his father's death in 1961 he became head of the Umma
Party (q.v.) and served as Prime Minister (1966-7).
The leader of the Ansar (q.v.) religious organization,
Sadiq's uncle al-Hadi, clashed with Sadiq and, for a time,
two branches of the al-Mahdi family (q.v.) and party opposed each other in parliament. Sadiq advocated a more
active modernization of the party and the Ansar organization than did Hadi. After the 1969 Revolution, Sadiq
was arrested and exiled, and has apparently been involved
in various attempts to overthrow the Numayri government.

MAHDI, SIDDIQ, al- see MAHDI, al-, FAMILY

MAHDI, al-, FAMILY. One of the major religious and political families in the modern Sudan. Its rise to promin-
ence began with the successful movement of Muhammad
Ahmad al-Mahdi (q.v.). The power of the family was
reduced somewhat during the time of the Khalifah Abdallahi (q.v.), who succeeded Muhammad Ahmad as leader of the Mahdist movement but was not a member of
the Mahdi's family. After the Anglo-Egyptian "reconquest" in 1899, Abd al-Rahman (q.v.), a son of the Mahdi, emerged as family leader and reorganized the Ansar
(q.v.) as a religious and political force. The Ansar became a Sudanese nationalist alternative to the influence
of Egypt and thus received some British encouragement.
The family provided leadership for both the Ansar religious organization and the Umma Party (q.v.). Abd al-
Rahman's son, Siddiq (1911-1961), was president of the
Umma Party and became the Imam of the Ansar when
Abd al-Rahman died in 1959. The family was divided
in the 1960's between a more modernist branch led by
the Umma Party president, Sadiq (q.v.), Siddiq's son,

and a traditionalist branch led by Hadi ibn Abd al-Rahman (1915-70), who had become Imam in 1961. Many members of the family held important posts in the Sudan. After the 1969 Revolution, the Mahdist family opposed the new regime and organized Ansar resistance to it. In the spring of 1970 there was an open military clash and the Ansar resistance was defeated. The Imam Hadi was killed in the fighting and most other members of the family fled into exile. Members of the family continue to be accused of plotting against the Numayri government.

MAHJUB, ABD AL-KHALIQ, d. 1971. Sudanese political leader. He was an active leader and early organizer in the Communist Party of the Sudan. He came to lead the more orthodox Marxist, Moscow-oriented section of the party. As Secretary General of the CPS he was jailed during the Abboud era and played an active role, after his release, in the 1964 Revolution. In 1968 he won a parliamentary seat running as an independent. Although he cooperated initially with the new regime after the 1969 Revolution, he was arrested and deported in 1970 and arrested again on his return. He was accused of cooperating with the attempted coup in July 1971 and was executed at that time.

MAHJUB, MUHAMMAD AHMAD, 1908- . Sudanese political leader and intellectual. He graduated from Gordon Memorial College and the Khartoum School of Law. He was active in the early intellectual groups, being a leader of the Hashmab group (q. v.) and writing articles and poetry. He was active in the Graduates Congress (q. v.) and, following World War II, he was secretary general of the Independence Front (q. v.). He was nominated to the Legislative Assembly (q. v.) but resigned in protest over a government pay raise. He served on the Constitutional Commission and in local government bodies. In 1953 he was elected to Parliament as an independent and was elected head of the parliamentary opposition by the pro-independence supporters. He thus became associated with the Umma Party (q. v.). He served as Minister of Foreign Affairs (1956-8) in the government of Abdallah Khalil (q. v.) and in the same post in the transition government after the 1964 Revolution. He was prime minister in 1965-6 and 1967-9 and played an active role in Arab world international relations. After the 1969 Revolution he spent much of his time out of the country writing.

MAJĀDHĪB. Plural of Majdhub. See MAJDHUBIYYAH.

MAJDHUB, al- see MAJDHUBIYYAH

MAJDHUBIYYAH. A localized tariqah (q.v.) associated with
the Majdhub family of Damar. The family and order
have a long tradition of religious and political influence.
The order is described as a branch of the Shadhiliyyah
(q.v.) because of the liturgy used by family leaders.
Muhammad al-Majdhub "al-Kabir" led the Majādhīb branch
of the Jaaliyyin tribe (q.v.) in the early 18th century.
His son, Hamad al-Majdhub (1693-1776), established the
family's position at Damar as leading educators, religious
leaders, and political intermediaries. The family's center became a virtually independent theocratic enclave.
Hamad's grandson, Muhammad al-Sughayyir (1796-1832),
transformed the order into one of regional rather than
localized importance. He fled from the Sudan after the
Turco-Egyptian armies destroyed Damar and studied in
Arabia. There he was a student of the Islamic revival-
ist, Ahmad ibn Idris (q.v.). On his return around 1830,
al-Sughayyir succeeded in winning followers throughout
the eastern Sudan. His nephew and khalifah (q.v.) was
al-Tahir al-Majdhub (1822-90). Al-Tahir joined the Mahdist movement in 1882 and he and his followers cooperated with Uthman Diqna (q.v.), the Mahdist commander.
The order did not dissolve during the Mahdist era and
al-Tahir's successor was his son, Muhammad al-Majdhub
III (1863-1930). Muhammad III fought as a Mahdist commander and received a pardon from the British. He was
a respected religious leader, poet, and scholar in the
early 20th-century. The family and order maintain a
position of prestige in the eastern and central Sudan, especially among some Beja Tribes (q.v.), but are less
involved in national politics. Leaders like Bashir Ahmad
Jalal al-Din (1854-1937), head of the order in the 1930's,
participated in local government and were influential land-
lords. Because of their association with the Mahdist
cause, the Majādhīb have often clashed with the Mirghani
family (q.v.).

MAKK (or MEKK). A title used by some tribal and local
chiefs in the Sudan.

MAKURIA. A kingdom which emerged in Nubia after the fall
of Meroe, capital of Kush (q.v.). Its capital was at Old

Dongola. In contrast to the neighboring states of Nobatia (q. v.) and Alwa (q. v.), the rulers of Makuria appear to have converted to Orthodox rather than Monophysite Christianity in the middle of the 6th-century. It merged with Nobatia to create the kingdom of Dongola (q. v.) around A. D. 650-700.

MALWAL, BONA. Sudanese journalist and political leader. Before the 1969 Revolution, he was editor of Vigilant, a Khartoum English-language newspaper with a southern perspective. After the Addis Ababa Agreement of 1972 (q. v.) he was named Deputy Minister of Information and Culture (1972-3), then Minister of State for Information (1973-6), and then Minister of Culture and Information (1976 into 1977).

MANJIL. A title used by exceptionally important chiefs subject to the Funj (q. v.) sultans. The best known manjils were the Abdallab (q. v.) chiefs.

MANSUR, IBRAHIM MONEIM. Sudanese businessman and political leader. He was named Minister of Economy and Trade in the first Sudan Socialist Union government in 1971. He served in the cabinet in that capacity until early 1975 when he lost his posts in the cabinet and the SSU Political Bureau as a result of questions of conflict of interest in the Peoples Assembly.

MA'QŪR, AHMAD, al-. A person associated in local traditions with the transfer of power in Darfur from the Tunjur (q. v.) to the Keira (q. v.). He is said to have been related through marriage to both dynasties. There is some question as to whether he is a fully historical figure or a mythological figure in whose story a long series of events is subsumed. The events of his life fit into the pattern of the "Wise Stranger," a common theme in the Sudanic belt of Africa, who comes to a barbarous land, introduces new ideas and customs, marries the chief's daughter, and establishes a new dynasty.

MARDI, MUHAMMAD AHMAD, al-, 1902-1966. Sudanese political leader. He was originally a judge in the Islamic Courts. He was elected to Parliament in 1953 with the NUP (q. v.) and became Minister of Local Government in Ismail al-Azhari's cabinet (1954-6). After the 1964 Revolution he was secretary general of the NUP and served in the cabinets of Muhammad Ahmad Mahjub (q. v.) and

and Sadiq al-Mahdi (q. v.) as Minister of Commerce
(1965-6).

MAY REVOLUTION. This revolution occurred in 1969. The
leaders of the new government were drawn from the military and were led by Ja'far al-Numayri (q. v.). The revolution brought an end to the period of party and parliamentary politics that had been initiated by the October
Revolution (q. v.) in 1964. Party political government
seemed unable to solve the problems of economic development and the war in the south. As a result, Sudanese
public opinion accepted the new revolutionary government
with little opposition.

MAYEN, GORDON MUORTAT. Southern political leader.
He joined the government service in 1946, eventually
serving as an assistant district commissioner. After
the 1964 Revolution he was the first vice president of
the Southern Front and Minister of Works in the transition government. He was a Southern Front (q. v.) spokesman at the Roundtable Conference in 1965 and then became active in southern exile groups. He served as foreign affairs spokesman for the Southern Sudan Provisional Government (q. v.) in 1968 but then formed the Nile
Provisional Government (q. v.) in opposition to the SSPG.
He advocated the policy of demanding complete independence for the south. When the NPG broke up, he did
not participate in the Anyidi Revolutionary Government
(q. v.) nor, later, did he cooperate with Joseph Lagu
(q. v.). He maintained his advocacy of total independence
for the south and rejected the Addis Ababa Agreement of
1972 (q. v.). He sought political asylum in Great Britain
and tried to create the African National Front.

MBORO, CLEMENT. Sudanese administrator and southern
political leader. He joined the government service in
1940 and was the senior southern Sudanese official in the
administration when the Sudan became independent. By
1964 he had become the deputy governor of Darfur Province. After the 1964 Revolution he was a founder and
the president of the Southern Front (q. v.) and was Minister of Interior in the transition government (1964-5).
He later served as Minister of Industry (1968-9) and was
elected to Parliament in 1968. He was jailed briefly
following the 1969 Revolution but was named president
of the Relief and Resettlement Commission after the Addis Ababa Agreement of 1972 (q. v.). He was elected to

the Southern Regional Peoples Assembly in 1973.

MEROE   see   KUSH

MIRGHANI, ALI IBN MUHAMMAD UTHMAN, al-, 1878-1968.
A major religious and political leader. He was a member of the Mirghani family (q.v.) and leader of the Khatmiyyah Tariqah (q.v.) in the 20th-century. He lived in Cairo during the Mahdist era and was a vigorous opponent of the Mahdi's movement. He cooperated with the British in the Anglo-Egyptian "reconquest" and was, in the early 20th-century, considered by the British to be the chief spokesman for local opinion. His rivalry with Abd al-Rahman al-Mahdi (q.v.) led him to be more sympathetic to Egyptian nationalism as the Mahdists received more favorable treatment from the British. Following World War II Sayyid Ali was the major patron for parties supporting unity of the Nile valley, especially the National Front (q.v.) (1949-52) and then the NUP (q.v.). After independence he supported the creation of the Peoples Democratic Party (q.v.) and opposed the politics of Ismail al-Azhari (q.v.). During the Abboud era his personal prestige among the military leaders meant that he maintained a degree of political influence. Following the 1964 Revolution illness reduced his direct involvement but he continued to be an important focus of political action until his death in 1968.

MIRGHANI, HASAN IBN MUHAMMAD UTHMAN, al- see
KHATMIYYAH and MIRGHANI FAMILY

MIRGHANI, MUHAMMAD UTHMAN, al- (and MUHAMMAD UTHMAN II) see KHATMIYYAH; MIRGHANI FAMILY

MIRGHANI, MUHAMMAD UTHMAN IBN AHMAD, al-. A member of the Mirghani family (q.v.). He assumed a leadership role in the family's center in Kassala after his father Ahmad's death in 1928. In national politics he usually accepted the leadership of his uncle, Ali al-Mirghani (q.v.). Muhammad Uthman was active in the early days of nationalist party politics and helped to organize the National Front (q.v.) in 1949, and was also the publisher of an independent newspaper later. However, he retired from public life in the 1950's because of ill health and some disagreements with other Khatmiyyah (q.v.) political leaders.

MIRGHANI, MUHAMMAD UTHMAN IBN ALI, al-, 1936- .
The leader of the Khatmiyyah (q.v.) after the death of
his father, Ali (q.v.), in 1968. As a young man he took
part in the religious and political activities of the order.
Following the Revolution of 1964 he participated more
directly in the Peoples Democratic Party (q.v.) and was
named to the Executive Committee of the Democratic
Unionist Party (q.v.) when it was formed in 1968 through
the merger of the PDP and the NUP (q.v.). After the
1969 Revolution he gave his support to the Numayri government in its conflict with the Ansar (q.v.) but has had
no public political role.

MIRGHANI FAMILY. A prominent family with religious prestige in the Sudan. In the 18th-century the family, re-
siding in Mecca, were among the recognized descendants
of the Prophet Muhammad. Muhammad Uthman al-Mirghani (1793-1853) was a student of Ahmad ibn Idris (q.v.)
and established the Khatmiyyah Tariqah (q.v.). Muhammad Uthman preached in the Sudan around 1817-21, where
he married a local woman. Hasan (1819-69), his son by
this marriage, returned to the Sudan and firmly established the family and order as an influential force in the Sudan. The family and order also had branches in Arabia,
Egypt, and Eritrea. The Mirghanis in the Sudan worked
closely with the Turco-Egyptian regime and were vigorous
opponents of the Mahdi. Hasan's son, Muhammad Uthman
II (1848-86) was an effective mediator and organizer. He
died in Cairo after leading ultimately unsuccessful resistance to the Mahdist movement in the Nile valley and Kassala area. His sons, Ahmad (1877-1928) and Ali (1878-
1968) (q.v.), lived outside the Sudan until the Anglo-
Egyptian reconquest. In the 20th-century many members
of the family, from different branches, were active in
religious and political affairs. They quite consistently
opposed revived Mahdist influence. At first they cooperated with the British but then became more pro-Egyptian,
fearing that British cooperation with Abd al-Rahman al-
Mahdi (q.v.) would lead to a Mahdist-dominated Sudan.
They aided parties supporting Nile valley unity. Muhammad Uthman ibn Ahmad (q.v.) helped organize the National Front (q.v.) in 1949, and the family, especially Ali,
was identified with the Peoples Democratic Party (q.v.)
formed in 1956. The family exercised some influence
on the Abboud regime and was relatively active in party
politics in the 1960's. At Ali al-Mirghani's death in 1968,

his son, Muhammad Uthman (q. v.) succeeded him in
family and tariqah leadership. The family cooperated
with the Numayri revolutionary government after the 1969
Revolution but it has not been as directly active or prominent as in previous years.

MIRGHANIYYAH   see   KHATMIYYAH

MONDIRI, IZBONI. Southern political leader. He was active
in southern party affairs in the 1950's, forming the Federal Party (q. v.) in 1957-8 as a result of a split within
the Liberal Party (q. v.). He was elected to Parliament
in 1958 but was jailed for incitement when he worked to
rally support for a federal form of government. After
the 1964 Revolution he was named Minister of Communications in the transition government but he left the country in 1965 to work with southern opposition groups. He
was a leader in the Azania Liberation Front (q. v.) and
was a prominent commander of southern forces in Equatoria. He was active in the South Sudan Liberation Movement (q. v.) and played a key role in the negotiations
leading up to the Addis Ababa Agreement of 1972 (q. v.).
After the settlement he served in the Southern Region
High Executive Council (1973-5).

MUFTI, IBRAHIM, al-, 1913- . A modern nationalist and
political leader. He was educated in the Sudan and became a lawyer. He was one of the founders of the Graduates Congress (q. v.) and the Ashigga Party (q. v.), and
was generally active in pro-Nile unity nationalism. He
became a member of the executive committee of the NUP
(q. v.) after it was formed in 1952 and was then elected
to Parliament. He served in the cabinet of Ismail al-
Azhari (q. v.) as Minister of Commerce and then of Finance. After the 1964 Revolution he was again a major
NUP leader, serving at various times as Minister of
Finance, of Foreign Affairs, and of Irrigation. He was
no longer active in politics after the 1969 Revolution.
He is a descendant of a 19th-century religious leader,
Ismail al-Wali (q. v.), and a cousin of Ismail al-Azhari.

MUHAMMAD ABU LIKAYLIK, ca. 1710-1776. A Funj (q. v.)
military commander who became the virtual ruler of the
sultanate. He won a series of battles and became the
governor of Kordofan. In 1761 he was joined by the old
Funj nobility and deposed Sultan Badi IV. He and his
family ruled through a series of puppet sultans. Although

his clan, the Hamaj (q. v.), dominated the state, they were unable to prevent a series of debilitating civil wars.

MUHAMMAD ALI, 1769-1849. A soldier from the Balkan Peninsula who was the Ottoman governor of Egypt between 1805-1849. He instituted modernizing reforms there and became virtually independent from his Ottoman overlords. In 1820 he sent military forces into the Sudan and conquered most of the northern part of the country. His governors established a relatively centralized regime and he himself visited the Sudan in 1838-9.

MUHAMMAD AL-MAHDI AL-SANUSI   see   SANUSIYYAH

MUHAMMAD AL-MAJDHUB AL-KABIR   see   MAJDHUBIYYAH

MUHAMMAD AL-MAJDHUB AL-SUGHAYYIR   see   MAJDHUB-
   IYYAH

MUHAMMAD BADR AL-UBAYD, ca. 1810-1884. A prominent religious leader in the Blue Nile area in the 19th-century. He was famous as a teacher and tariqah (q. v.) leader and established an important religious center at Umm Dibban. His sons gave strong support to the Mahdist movement.

MUHAMMAD IBN SARHAN AL-SUGHAYRUN   see   AWLAD
   JABIR

MUHAMMAD KHUSRAW AL-DAFTARDAR, d. 1833. A Turkish soldier in Muhammad Ali's (q. v.) service in Egypt. He was a financial officer and then a major officer in the armies that conquered the Sudan in 1820-22. He was responsible for the conquest of Kordofan and also crushed the revolt that broke out in 1822 following the murder of Ismail Kamil (q. v.). He returned to Egypt in 1824.

MUHAMMAD SHARIF NŪR AL-DĀ'IM, d. 1908. Leader of the Sammaniyyah (q. v.) in the 19th-century and grandson of Ahmad al-Tayyib, who introduced the order into the Sudan. Muhammad Sharif was a prominent religious notable in the time of Turco-Egyptian rule. His most famous student was Muhammad Ahmad al-Mahdi (q. v.). Although Muhammad Sharif quarreled with his student and initially opposed the Mahdist movement, he later joined the Mahdists. After the Anglo-Egyptian conquest, Muhammad Sharif lived in the village of Ahmad al-Tayyib's tomb as a respected figure. He was succeeded in Sam-

maniyyah leadership after his death by his son, Abd al-
Mahmud.

MUHAMMAD TAJ AL-DIN AL-BAHARI see QADIRIYYAH

MUSA, UMAR AL-HAJJ. Sudanese soldier and political leader. He completed training at the Officers Training School
in Omdurman in 1944 and began a military career. During the Abboud era he was appointed officer commanding
the Signal Corps and was a senior officer at the time of
the 1969 Revolution. Soon after the revolution he was
Minister of Defense briefly and then was named Minister
of National Guidance (1969-71), becoming Minister of Information and Culture in the first SSU cabinet in 1971,
remaining in the post until 1975. In 1975 he was made
Assistant Secretary General of the Sudan Socialist Union.

MUSLIM BROTHERHOOD. A militant religious and political
organization formed in Egypt in 1928. It advocates government and laws based directly on the Qur'an and works
for fundamentalist Islamic revival. The Brotherhood recruited individual Sudanese in the 1940's but a branch was
not established in the Sudan until the early 1950's. At
that time the Brotherhood came together with the Islamic
Movement for Liberation, a Sudanese group with similar
aims formed in 1949. The Brotherhood was popular a-
mong students and recent graduates. In 1964 it entered
electoral politics with the creation of the Islamic Charter
Front, an attempt to build a mass organization around
the Brotherhood nucleus. The leader was Hasan al-
Turabi from the University of Khartoum Faculty of Law.
There were some divisions among the leadership in the
1960's reflecting tensions between leaders of the local
Islamic Movement for Liberation and the Brotherhood.
All of these Islamic groups were outlawed after the 1969
Revolution and some have been active in opposing the
revolutionary regime.

MUSTAFA, ZAKI. Sudanese lawyer and legal scholar. He
served for a time as Dean of the Law Faculty at the
University of Khartoum and was named Attorney General
in 1973. In 1975 he became a part-time legal advisor
to Numayri (q.v.) and was appointed secretary general
of the joint Saudi-Sudanese authority for exploitation of
Red Sea resources.

-N-

NAPATA. Site of a great temple to Amon built during the
New Kingdom in Egypt. During the "Libyan" 22nd Dynasty in Egypt (ca. 950 B.C.), much of the Amon priesthood
moved to Napata and a distinctive Egyptian-Kushite culture emerged. Napata was the capital of the kingdom of
Kush (q.v.) until the city's destruction during the invasion
of Psammetichus II in 591 B.C.

NATIONAL FRONT, 1949-1952. A political party formed in
1949 by members of the Khatmiyyah (q.v.) and received
support from Ali al-Mirghani (q.v.). It opposed the more
extreme positions of the Ashigga (q.v.), favoring dominion status for the Sudan in unity with Egypt. The leader
of the Front was Muhammad Uthman ibn Ahmad al-Mirghani (q.v.), a nephew of Sayyid Ali, and its major political spokesman was Mirghani Hamza (q.v.). The party
was weakened by the illness of Muhammad Uthman in
1952 and was dissolved when the Front participated in
the creation of the NUP (q.v.).

NATIONAL FRONT, 1957-1958. A group of organizations
opposed to the pro-Western and conservative policies of
the Abdallah Khalil (q.v.) government. It was formed
in 1957 and included the NUP (q.v.), the Anti-Imperialist
Front (q.v.), and the National Union of Students. The
Front came to an end with the military government of
1958.

NATIONAL FRONT, 1974. A combination of Muslim Brotherhood (q.v.), Umma Party (q.v.) and other politicians
opposed to the Numayri regime, accused of anti-govern-
ment plots.

NATIONAL PARTY, 1952 see ABD AL-RAHMAN AL-HINDI

NATIONAL UNIONIST PARTY (NUP). The NUP was formed
late in 1952 as a merger of a variety of groups favoring
unity of the Nile valley. It received the support of Ali
al-Mirghani (q.v.) and was led by Ismail al-Azhari (q.v.).
It won a majority of seats in the parliament elected in
1953 and formed the government that proclaimed Sudan's
independence. However, in 1956 the Khatmiyyah (q.v.)
wing of the NUP left to form the Peoples Democratic
Party (PDP), leaving the NUP as the party of al-Azhari.

It was outlawed during the Abboud regime and joined in opposition. After the 1964 Revolution, al-Azhari allied his party with the Umma Party (q.v.), with al-Azhari acting as head of state and the Umma providing the prime ministers. The NUP merged with the PDP to form the Democratic Unionist Party in 1967.

NATIONALIST PARTY (Hizb al-Qawmiyyin). A short-lived party created in 1946 supporting independence for the Sudan. It participated in the National Front (q.v.) and soon merged with the Umma Party (q.v.).

NAZIR. The Arabic term for "director." In the Sudan in local administration the term was used for the head of a large tribal group.

NIAM NIAM. An older term, usually applied to the Azande (q.v.).

NILE PARTY. A small party formed in 1967. It had some following in Bahr al-Ghazal and won one seat in the 1968 parliamentary elections.

NILE PROVISIONAL GOVERNMENT (NPG). A southern political group. It was formed in Uganda in 1969 when the Southern Sudan Provisional Government (q.v.) broke up. Its leaders were Gordon Mayen (q.v.) and Maro Morgan. The NPG was soon split with the formation of the Anyidi Revolutionary Government (q.v.). The NPG dissolved in 1970 but Mayen refused to accept the leadership of Joseph Lagu (q.v.) in the Southern Sudan Liberation Movement. Mayen formed the African National Front which opposed the 1972 settlement.

NILO-HAMITIC see NILOTES

NILOTES. A grouping of tribes in the southern Sudan. The first migrations of these peoples into the Sudan may have been more than 1,000 years ago, and they have spread throughout the southern region from a core area in Bahr al-Ghazal. Cattle-herding pastoralism is the basis for Nilotic tribal life. Nilotes speak Eastern Sudanic languages, a subfamily of the Chari-Nile branch of the Nilo-Saharan language family. They include the groups called Nilo-Hamites in older anthropological terminology. The three largest Nilotic tribes are the Dinka, Nuer, and Shilluk.

NIMR MUHAMMAD NIMR, ca. 1785-ca. 1846.   The last of the
  autonomous Makks of the Jaaliyin (q. v.) in Shendi.   He
  rose to power in the warfare of the last days of the Funj
  (q. v.) and unwillingly submitted to the Turco-Egyptian
  army in 1821.   In 1822 he murdered Ismail Kamil (q. v.),
  the Egyptian commander, but his revolt was short-lived.
  He fled to the Ethiopian borderlands and lived as a ban-
  dit for the rest of his life.

NOBATIA.   A kingdom which emerged in Lower Nubia in the
  late A. D. 200's.   The origins of the Nobatae are unclear
  but they seem to have received assistance from the Roman rulers of Egypt in conflict with the Blemmyes (q. v.).
  It is probable that the Nobatae were the people of the
  X-Group (q. v.) or Ballana Culture (q. v.) but some scholars identify the latter as the Blemmyes.   Nobatae and
  Blemmyes joined together at times to fight the Romans.
  The rulers of Nobatia converted to Monophysite Christianity through the works of Julian (q. v.) around A. D. 543.
  The kingdom eventually merged with Makuria (q. v.) to
  form the kingdom of Dongola (q. v.) around A. D. 650-700.

NUBA.   A variety of peoples who live in the Nuba Mountains
  areas of southern Kordofan.   They may originally have
  come from the Nile valley and central plains areas.   They
  have maintained distinctive linguistic and cultural traditions but have been increasingly incorporated into northern Sudanese life.   Nuba have been active in the Sudanese military.   Occasional Nuba political activism can be
  seen in movements like the General Union of Nubas (q. v.)
  led by Phillip Abbas Gaboush (q. v.).

NUBIA.   The area in the Nile valley south of Aswan in Egypt
  extending into the northern Sudan.   In ancient history it
  is the area of Kush (q. v.).   By the time of the fall of
  the medieval Christian kingdoms, the population had become almost completely Muslim.   Although many Nubians
  speak Arabic, the Nubian languages have been maintained,
  with a number of local dialects being spoken.   Nubians
  have been active in trade and politics.   Many have left
  the home area but maintain a close sense of community
  in the cities and towns of Egypt and the Sudan where
  they have settled.   As a result of the inundation of land
  caused by the building of the High Dam at Aswan many
  Nubians have been resettled.   More than 30,000 were
  moved to Khashm al-Girbah (q. v.) in the eastern Sudan
  in the 1960's.   Because of a relatively high level of ed-

ucation and active involvement, Nubians have played an
important role in modern Sudanese politics.

NUER.   A major group of Nilotes (q. v.) concentrated along
the White Nile.   Although they have a homogeneous tribal culture, they do not have strongly centralized political institutions.   They have a warlike reputation and vigorously resisted British control early in the 20th-century.
They were less active in later political developments,
although Buth Diu (q. v.), an important southern politician
after World War II, was a Nuer.   The tribe was described by the anthropologist E. E. Evans-Pritchard.

NUMAYRI, JA'FAR, 1930- . Sudanese political leader and
soldier.   He graduated from the Sudan Military College
in 1952 and took military training courses in Germany
and the United States.   He became officer commanding
in the military training camp at Gebeit in the Red Sea
area.   He was the recognized leader of the revolution
in May 1969, and became the chairman of the Council
of the Revolution and Minister of Defense in the new government.   In October 1969 he became Prime Minister
and has held that post, along with a variety of minister-
ial positions, since then.   In 1970 the Revolutionary
Council named him Supreme Commander of the Armed
Forces.   In July 1971 he was briefly dismissed during
an abortive coup attempt but he soon regained his position.   In the fall of 1971 he was elected President in a
special national referendum and held the positions of
President, Prime Minister, and Minister of Planning in
the first government formed after the adoption of the new
national constitution.   He was also a member of the SSU
Political Bureau.   He is recognized as the leading figure
in the creation of the new constitutional regime, the organization of the Sudan Socialist Union, and in bringing
about the negotiations that led to a settlement of the conflict in the southern Sudan.   In 1977 he remained the
leader of the May Revolution and the movements that it
had initiated in the Sudan.

NUR AL-DIN, MUHAMMAD, 1897- . Economist and political leader from Sudanese Nubia.   He worked for the
National Bank of Egypt, serving in various branches in
the Sudan (1925-47).   He was active in early nationalist
politics, acting as president of the Graduates Club in
El-Obeid, and helping to found the Graduates Congress
(q. v.).   He was vice president of the Ashigga Party (q. v.)

when it was formed and then led a faction of that party
that disagreed at times with Ismail al-Azhari (q.v.). He
became an officer of the NUP (q.v.) when it was formed
and was elected to Parliament in 1953. He was active
in supporting unity with Egypt and opposed Azhari's movement toward an independent Sudan.

-O-

OCTOBER REVOLUTION.   This revolution occurred in 1964
and resulted in the ouster of Ibrahim Abboud (q.v.),
bringing an end to the first period of military rule in
the independent Sudan.   It was accomplished through civilian demonstrations and general dissatisfaction with the
Abboud regime.

ODUHO, JOSEPH.   Southern schoolmaster and political leader.
He taught school in Equatoria and then was elected to
Parliament in 1958.   He fled from the Sudan and was one
of the founders of the Sudan African National Union (SANU)
(q.v.) and was its president.   As SANU broke up, he
helped to form the Azania Liberation Front (q.v.) in 1966
and continued to be active in southern resistance.   After
the Addis Ababa Agreement of 1972 (q.v.) he returned to
the Sudan and served as a member of the Southern Region High Executive Council (1972-5) and the SSU Political Bureau (1974-5).   He was also elected to the Southern Regional Peoples Assembly in 1973.

OSMAN DIGNA   see   UTHMAN DIQNA

-P-

PALEOLITHIC, SUDANESE.   Some of the major paleolithic
tool industries and their sites in the Sudan are: (1)
Nubian Mousterian, Type A, from 47,000-35,000 years
B.P. (before present); found in a site east of Wadi Halfa.
(2) Khor Musan, 22,000-18,700 B.P.; found in a site at
Dibeira East, Nubia.   (3) Halfan, 20,000-17,000 B.P.;
found at a site at Wadi Halfa.   (4) Sebilian, 15,000-
11,000 B.P.; found at a site near Mirgissa, Wadi Halfa.
(5) Qadan, 14,500-6,400 B.P.; found at a site in Halfa
Dequim, south of Wadi Halfa.

PASHA.   The highest title or rank in the old Turkish or
Egyptian court and military hierarchy.

PAYSAMA, STANISLAUS, 1903- . Sudanese political leader and administrator. He was born in Fashir, Darfur, and educated in mission schools. He entered government service in 1927, serving in a variety of administrative posts. After World War II he assisted in the formation of the Southern Sudan Welfare Committee (q.v.) and was in the Legislative Assembly (q.v.) for Bahr al-Ghazal. He served on the Constitutional Commission. He helped to organize the Southern Party and became president of the party after it changed its name to the Liberal Party (q.v.) in 1954. He became involved in a leadership contest within the party with Benjamin Lwoki (q.v.) but retained control. He served in the Parliament from 1954-8. After the 1964 Revolution he formed a party called the Liberal Party which had little success in elections and minimal political influence.

PEOPLES DEMOCRATIC PARTY (PDP). A party formed in 1956 by Khatmiyyah elements in the National Unionist Party (q.v.). It received the support of Ali al-Mirghani (q.v.) and was led by Ali Abd al-Rahman (q.v.). In 1956 it joined with the Umma Party (q.v.) to form a coalition government replacing that of Ismail al-Azhari (q.v.). This coalition continued until the Abboud coup in 1958, after which all parties were outlawed. The PDP included a wide spectrum of political views, ranging from those of conservative rural leaders to some of the most radical politicians in the Sudan. The PDP leadership participated in opposition to Abboud and in the 1964 Revolution, but it then boycotted the 1965 elections. In 1967 the PDP merged with the NUP to form the Democratic Unionist Party (q.v.).

PIANKHI. A ruler of Kush (q.v.) who completed the conquest of Egypt begun by his father, Kashta (q.v.). His long reign over Egypt and Kush (751-716 B.C.) provided the basis for the Kushite 25th Dynasty in Egypt.

PROFESSIONAL FRONT see FRONT OF PROFESSIONAL ORGANIZATIONS

-Q-

QADI. A Muslim judge who administers Islamic law.

QADIRIYYAH. The oldest and possibly most widespread

tariqah (q.v.) in the Islamic world. It is traced back
to Abd al-Qadir al-Jaylani (died 1166) in Baghdad. The
order is decentralized with local leadership having independence regarding rules and practices. The order is
traditionally said to have been brought to the Sudan in
the 16th-century by Muhammad Taj al-Din al-Bahari
(ca. 1520-ca. 1600). He came from Baghdad and taught
for seven years. The khalifahs (q.v.) that he appointed
became major religious leaders in the Sudan and their
descendants include prominent holy families like the Arakiyyin (q.v.) and the Ya'qubab (q.v.). Other famous
Qadiriyyah saints, like Idris ibn al-Arbab (q.v.), affil-
iated with the order through their own travels or experience. The tariqah's influence in the Sudan is tied to
the prestige of individual local leaders. It is strongest
in the Gezira area, where the clans of early saints are
located, but it also is important in nomadic tribal areas.
Its flexibility of organization has sometimes made the
order an effective missionary group through its ability
to adapt to local conditions.

QARĪB ALLĀH SĀLIH AL-TAYYIB, 1866-1936. A leader of
the Sammaniyyah Tariqah (q.v.) in the 20th-century. He
was a descendant of Ahmad al-Tayyib who brought the
order to the Sudan in 1800. He succeeded his cousin,
Abd al-Mahmud, the son of Muhammad Sharif Nur al-
Da'im (q.v.), as khalifah (q.v.) in 1915. Qarīb Allāh
had studied in Egypt and the Hejaz and was widely respected for his piety. His personal followers came to
comprise a special branch of the Sammaniyyah known as
the Qarībiyyah.

QARIBĪYYAH   see   QARĪB ALLĀH SĀLIH AL-TAYYIB

-R-

RABIH ZUBAYR, 1845-1900. Slave trader and adventurer.
He was born in Khartoum and worked in the southern
provinces as a slave trader. He gradually moved west-
ward, later claiming to be a follower of the Mahdist
movement, and attempted to establish states in Chad
and Bornu. After a series of wars he was killed by
the French in 1900 near Lake Chad.

RASHID, IBRAHIM, al- see RASHIDIYYAH

RASHIDIYYAH. A tariqah (q.v.) founded by Ibrahim al-
Rashid al-Diwayhi (died 1874). Ibrahim came from a
Shayqiyyah clan near Dongola and was a disciple of Ahmad
ibn Idris (q.v.). He claimed to be the true khalifah
(q.v.) of his teacher but this claim was disputed by leaders of the Khatmiyyah (q.v.) and other followers of Ahmad. Ibrahim won some followers in the Sudan but his
most successful ministry was among pilgrims in Mecca.
The order gained adherents from India, Arabia, Syria,
and Somaliland, where it was reported to be the order
of the reforming Muslim leader, Muhammad ibn Abdallah
(called the "Mad Mulla" in some Western literature),
early in the 20th-century. Ibrahim died in Mecca but
the order was continued in the Sudan on a small scale
under local leadership.

[1]REPUBLICAN PARTY (al-hizb al-jumhuri). A small but
relatively long-lived party founded in 1945 by Mahmud
Muhammad Taha. It favored Sudanese independence but
did not ally itself with any other party or front. The
party had no electoral success but continued to be represented in all-party consultative groups like the National
Constitutional Committee in 1956. During the Abboud regime the party's founder and leader became more active
in the cause of Islamic reform and the movement emerged in non-party form following the 1964 Revolution. Mahmud Muhammad Taha has written a number of books on
religious and social subjects and these provide the basis
for the group's programs.

[2]REPUBLICAN PARTY. During 1946 a second party named
the Republican Party was created by Yusuf al-Tinay, but
it was very short-lived.

-S-

SAID, BESHIR MOHAMMED, 1921- . Sudanese journalist.
He was educated at the University of Khartoum and in
Great Britain. He then worked in the Publications Bureau of the Ministry of Education (1947-54). In 1954 he
started al-Ayyam press, which published a major independent newspaper and other things. He served for a
time as president of the Sudanese Press Association and
also worked in the Office of Public Information in the
United Nations Secretariat (1961-3). After the 1969 Revolution he was held in detention for a time.

SALIM QAPUDAN. A Turkish sailor who commanded three
    expeditions attempting to discover the source of the
    White Nile in 1839-42.

SAMMANIYYAH. A tariqah (q.v.) organized by Muhammad
    al-Samman (1718-75) in Arabia. It was brought to the
    Sudan by Ahmad al-Tayyib al-Bashir (1742-1824), a mem-
    ber of a Sudanese holy family who had traveled and stud-
    ied in Egypt and the Hejaz. He built a large following
    for the tariqah in the central Sudan. His grandson, Mu-
    hammad Sharif Nur al-Da'im (q.v.), was a teacher of
    Muhammad Ahmad al-Mahdi (q.v.), who was a recognized
    member of the order. The Sammaniyyah provided many
    followers for the Mahdi, but the tariqah did not dissolve
    or simply become a branch of the Mahdist movement.
    In the 20th-century the order continued to have a large
    number of followers in the central Sudan and also devel-
    oped branch orders which became influential. The most
    notable of these are the followers of Yusuf al-Hindi (q.v.)
    and Qarib Allah Salih (q.v.).

SANUSIYYAH. The tariqah (q.v.) established by Muhammad
    ibn Ali al-Sanusi (1791-1859), a student of Ahmad ibn
    Idris (q.v.). The founder created a strong base for re-
    ligious and political influence in Libya. His son, Mu-
    hammad al-Mahdi al-Sanusi (1844-1902), was invited by
    the Sudanese Mahdi to be one of his high officers, or
    khalifahs, but the Sanusi declined. In the early 20th-
    century the Sanusiyyah was seen as a Pan-Islamic in-
    fluence and was believed to be the force behind a number
    of revolts in the Sudan. The order has limited influence
    in the Sudan, primarily among immigrants from the west
    and in Darfur.

SATURNINO, LOHURE, d. 1967. Southern political leader
    and Roman Catholic priest. He was named to the con-
    stitutional committee in 1957 and elected to Parliament
    in 1958, becoming a leading member in the southern
    parliamentary bloc. After the Abboud coup in 1958 he
    returned to the south and then fled from the country in
    1961. He was one of the creators of the Sudan African
    National Union (q.v.) and helped to organize Anya Nya
    activities. After SANU broke up, he became one of the
    prominent members of the Azania Liberation Front (q.v.).
    He was killed early in 1967 near the Uganda border.

SAYYID (or SAYYED). A title or form of address. It us-

ually denotes a position of religious prestige but is sometimes used as the equivalent of "mister." To find a
name beginning with "Sayyid," look under the names following the title. For example, to find "Sayyid Abd al-
Rahman al-Mahdi," look under "Mahdi."

SETU. An independent Nubian kingdom in the 3rd millennium B. C.

SHADHILIYYAH. A major tariqah (q.v.) traced back to the
teachings of Abu al-Hasan Ali al-Shadhili (1196-1258).
The founder was a wandering teacher and his tariqah is
more a set of liturgies and a school of thought than a
socio-political organization. Its prayers and liturgies
are used by many tariqahs in the Sudan. Some of these,
like the Majdhubiyyah (q.v.), are considered branches
of the order, while others, like the Khatmiyyah (q.v.),
are independent.

SHAHEINAB. An early neolithic site near modern Khartoum.
There was no evidence of plant domestication but some
for the domestication of animals, especially a dwarf goat.
The culture may be related to cultures found in Tibesti
and Fayyum. Carbon dates for Shaheinab materials of
3100 B. C. and 3500 B. C. have been determined.

SHANNAN, ABD AL-RAHIM MUHAMMAD KHAYR. Sudanese
soldier and political figure. During the era of the government of Ibrahim Abboud (q.v.) Shannan was active in
the Revolutionary Command Council and then was arrested and jailed for plotting against Abboud. He was released after the 1964 Revolution and was elected to Parliament (1965-8) and formally retired from the army.
In 1973 he was arrested for plotting against the regime
of Ja'far Numayri (q.v.) in association with conservative
opposition to the regime. He was convicted but given a
light sentence because of poor health and advanced age.

SHARIA. The Arabic term for the body of Islamic law.

SHAWQISTS. The group associated with Muhammad Afandi
Shawqi in the Graduates Club during the 1920's and 1930's.
Abd al-Rahman al-Mahdi (q.v.) supported the group, which
mistrusted Egypt and favored the idea of a separate, in-
dependent Sudan. Its major opponents in the Graduates
Club were the Filists (q.v.).

SHAYKH (also often spelled sheikh, sheik, shaikh). A tribal,
family, or clan leader. The title is also used for religious leaders and teachers.

SHAYKH, SHAFIEH AHMAD, al- see SUDAN WORKERS
TRADE UNION FEDERATION

SHAYQIYYAH. A major Arab tribe usually said to be part
of the Jaaliyyin group (q. v.). The tribe was centered
in the Nile valley south of Dongola and established a
series of independent tribal kingdoms in the later Funj
(q. v.) period. After vigorously resisting the Turco-
Egyptian invasion, the Shayqiyyah cooperated with the
new rulers and spread throughout the Sudan as irregular
soldiers and traders. They actively opposed the Mahdiyyah and suffered great losses. As a tribe they were too
disintegrated to have much power, but as individuals and
families, they have been prominent in 20th-century history.

SHIBEIKA, MEKKI. Sudanese intellectual leader and university professor. He graduated from the American University of Beirut and received his doctorate from London
University in history. He taught in Gordon College and
then in the University of Khartoum. He was active in
the organization of the Graduates Congress (q. v.) and
served as its secretary for a time. After independence
he became professor of history at the University of Khartoum and then served for a time as Dean of the Faculty
of Arts and also as president of the Philosophical Society
of the Sudan. He has written many important studies of
Sudanese history in both English and Arabic.

SHIBLI, AMIN. Sudanese lawyer and political leader. He
was active in the 1964 Revolution and served for a number of years as president of the Sudan Bar Association.
He was an organizer of a new Socialist Party in 1967
which hoped to be able to attract a broader basis of public support than the Communist Party of the Sudan (q. v.)
had won. He served briefly as Minister of Justice after
the 1969 Revolution and then in a variety of posts representing the Sudan in the Arab League and other organizations.

SHILLUK. A major group of Nilotes (q. v.) concentrated a-
long with White Nile in the Fashoda area. They are
less pastoral than other Nilotes and engage in settled

agricultural life. Shilluk political organization is centralized around a king or reth and this has given the tribe
greater unity than is found among the Dinka (q. v.) or
Nuer (q. v.).

SHINGEITI, MUHAMMAD SALIH, d. 1968. Sudanese political
leader and business man. He served for many years in
the administrative service and was active in early nationalist movements. He was a part of the Sudan Union Society (q. v.) and was active in the formation of the Graduates Congress (q. v.). He was a political independent
but usually worked closely with Abd al-Rahman al-Mahdi
(q. v.). He was speaker of the Legislative Assembly
(q. v.) and the House of Representatives in the first Parliament, elected in 1953. During the Abboud era he was
actively involved in agricultural businesses and other commercial ventures. After the 1964 Revolution he worked
with the Umma Party (q. v.) but was not as directly involved in politics as before. He was nominated by Sadiq
al-Mahdi's (q. v.) wing of the Umma Party to the Supreme
Council but was not elected. He died on return from pilgrimage to Mecca in 1968.

SHUKRIYYAH. A great Arab tribe in the Juhayna (q. v.)
group. They are concentrated in the Blue Nile and Kassala areas and are a major camel-herding tribe. The
fortunes and history of the tribe are reflected in the experience of the leading family of the tribe, the Abu Sinn
family (q. v.).

SHUQAYR, NA'ŪM BEY, 1863-1922. A Syrian Christian who
worked in the intelligence department of the Egyptian
Army and then in the Sudan. He was influential as an
advisor on local affairs for the British in the Sudan. His
history of the Sudan (Tārīkh al-Sūdān) is one of the major sources for Sudanese history, especially for the Mahdist period.

SINGA SKULL. A paleolithic skull among the earliest human
remains found in the Sudan, dating to about 17, 000 years
ago. The skull, found in the Blue Nile area, is thought
to belong to a proto-Bushman type of person.

SLATIN PASHA, BARON RUDOLF VON, 1857-1932. Austrian officer who served in the Egyptian and Sudanese
services. After a varied military career, he became an
administrator in the Turco-Egyptian government in the

Sudan.   The Mahdist revolt broke out while he was governor of Darfur and he was captured.   He was a prisoner
for eleven years and came to know the Khalifah Abdallahi
al-Ta'ishi (q.v.) very well.   He escaped in 1895 and
worked in Egyptian-British military intelligence.   After
the establishment of British control in the Sudan he was
named inspector-general and had great influence over policies relating to local affairs.   Because of his Austrian
nationality he resigned his post at the beginning of World
War I and left the Sudanese governmental service.

SOCIALIST PARTY OF THE SUDAN   see   COMMUNIST
    PARTY OF THE SUDAN

SOCIALIST REPUBLIC PARTY (SRP).   A political party form-
    ed in 1951 by tribal leaders and moderate intellectuals.
    The SRP supported independence but feared a Mahdist
    monarchy.   It also opposed direct political involvement
    by the religious organizations.   The SRP cooperated with
    the British and was believed by some Sudanese to have
    been a British creation.   Its leadership included a num-
    ber of important tribal and rural leaders.   The SRP sec-
    retary was the moderate intellectual Ibrahim Badri.   How-
    ever, the party was opposed by the Umma Party (q.v.),
    the pro-Egyptian groups, and the religious leaders.   It
    won only three parliamentary seats in the elections of
    1953 and soon ended formal activity.

SOUTH SUDAN LIBERATION MOVEMENT   see   ANYA NYA

SOUTHERN FRONT.   A coalition of southerners formed in
    1964.   It drew upon southern civil servants and operated
    within the Sudan rather than in exile.   It had three min-
    isterial posts in the 1964-5 transition government and won
    10 seats in the 1968 parliamentary elections.   Front lead-
    ers included Clement Mboro (q.v.) and Hilary Logali
    (q.v.).   The Front was dissolved after the 1969 Revolu-
    tion.

SOUTHERN LIBERAL PARTY   see   LIBERAL PARTY
    (Southern)

SOUTHERN PARTY.   A party formed by educated southerners
    just prior to the 1953 elections.   It had broad support in
    the south, winning 12 of the 22 southern seats in the
    House of Representatives in those elections.   In 1954
    the party changed its name to the Liberal Party (q.v.).

SOUTHERN SUDAN ASSOCIATION. A London-based organization of southern Sudanese formed in 1970. It published
the Grass Curtain, a magazine which hoped to influence
Western opinion in favor of the southern cause. It had
ties with Anya Nya (q. v.) and was dissolved after the
Addis Ababa Agreement of 1972 (q. v.). Its director,
Madeng de Garang (q. v.), became a member of the new
Southern Region High Executive Committee which was
created as a result of the settlement.

SOUTHERN SUDAN PROVISIONAL GOVERNMENT (SSPG).
A southern political organization created in 1967. It
basically replaced the Azania Liberation Front (q. v.)
and was an attempt to bring together all the southern
groups existing outside the Sudan. It opposed southern
groups that participated in the Sudanese political system.
Aggrey Jaden (q. v.) was president of the SSPG. The
SSPG disintegrated by March 1969 due to personality
conflicts and tribal rivalries. It was succeeded by the
Nile Provisional Government (q. v.).

SOUTHERN SUDAN WELFARE COMMITTEE. An early southern organization formed in 1946-7 by Stanislaus Paysama
(q. v.) and others. It was primarily composed of southerners in government services concerned about equal pay
and opportunity with northerners.

STEINER, ROLF. Mercenary of German origin. He had
been in the French Foreign Legion and then was involved
in a wide variety of military ventures as a mercenary
soldier. He was arrested in 1971 in Uganda and was
turned over to the Sudan to stand trial as a mercenary
aiding the southerners. He was convicted but his death
sentence was commuted to 20 years' imprisonment. He
was released in 1974.

SUDAN AFRICAN CLOSED DISTRICTS NATIONAL UNION
(SACDNU) see SUDAN AFRICAN NATIONAL UNION

SUDAN AFRICAN LIBERATION FRONT (SALF). A southern
political organization formed by Aggrey Jaden (q. v.) in
1965 following the breakup of the Sudan African National
Union (q. v.). Later in the year SALF merged with the
Azania Liberation Front (q. v.).

SUDAN AFRICAN NATIONAL UNION (SANU). A southern
liberation movement formed in exile during the Abboud

period. William Deng (q. v.), Joseph Oduho (q. v.) and
Father Saturnino (q. v.) were among the organizers in
1962. It was originally called the Sudan African Closed
Districts National Union and changed its name to SANU
in 1963. SANU leadership split during and after the
Roundtable Conference of 1965 in Khartoum. The issue
was the degree of compromise possible with the Sudanese
government. William Deng remained in the Sudan. His
"SANU-Inside" contested elections and won 10 southern
seats in Parliament in 1967 and 15 seats in the 1968 e-
lections. Its support was concentrated in Bahr al-Ghazal.
In 1967-8 SANU-Inside split into factions led by William
Deng and Alfred Wol. The murder of Deng in 1968 reduced the influence of SANU-Inside. After 1965 most of
the leaders of "SANU-in-exile" formed the Azania Liberation Front (q. v.).

SUDAN MOVEMENT FOR NATIONAL LIBERATION   see
    COMMUNIST PARTY OF THE SUDAN

SUDAN PARTY (Hizb al-Sudan). A short-lived political party
    formed in 1952 by Muhammad Ahmad Umar. Its platform
    was virtually unique in that it called for an independent
    Sudan as a member of the British Commonwealth.

SUDAN UNION SOCIETY (al-Ittihad). An early nationalist
    organization formed in Omdurman around 1920. It was
    a secret group containing a number of men, like Abdallah
    Khalil (q. v.) and Muhammad Salih Shingeiti (q. v.), who
    were later important political leaders. It opposed the
    British administration and worked for Sudanese self-de-
    termination. Some members left the Union and joined
    the more militant White Flag League (q. v.), and most
    of the Union's formal activities ceased as a result of
    the suppression of nationalism after 1924.

SUDAN UNITED TRIBES ASSOCIATION. An association form-
    ed by Ali Abd al-Latif (q. v.) advocating Sudanese inde-
    pendence. When he was jailed in 1922 the Association
    came to an end. After his release from jail in 1923,
    Ali formed the White Flag League (q. v.).

SUDAN UNITY PARTY   see   DENG, SANTINO

SUDAN WORKERS TRADE UNION FEDERATION (SWTUF).
    A congress of trade unions in the Sudan formed in 1950
    as an outgrowth of the Workers Congress of 1949. It

was activist in nationalist causes and organized many
strikes before independence. It continued to represent
militant and radical unionism after independence. It
came into conflict with the Abboud regime but survived
the first era of military rule. Official government recognition was granted in 1966 but was withdrawn after
1969, although combined union action has continued. The
SWTUF had a long and close association with the Communist Party of the Sudan (q.v.), especially through the
long-term secretary general of SWTUF, Shafieh Ahmad
al-Shaykh. His execution in 1971 accelerated the decline
of the Federation's influence.

SUDANESE SOCIALIST UNION (SSU). The political organization of the Numayri regime. It was established in
1971 along the lines of the socialist unions in Egypt and
Syria. The SSU is the only officially recognized political association in the Sudan and is the basis for the national assembly and the constitutional structure. It also
contains a group of popular organizations like the Women's Union, that replace earlier professional, labor,
and interest group associations.

SUDD. The large swamp region in the southern Sudan. It
is in the Bahr al-Jabal part of the White Nile, in a flat
area where swamp vegetation makes navigation of the
river impossible without constant clearing activity.

SUFI. The Arabic term for a Muslim mystic.

SUGHAYYIRUN, MUHAMMAD, al- see AWLAD JABIR

SULAYMAN, AHMAD. Sudanese lawyer and political leader.
He was an active member of the Communist Party of the
Sudan, serving at times on its executive committee. He
was Minister of Agriculture in the transition government
after the 1964 Revolution and was elected to Parliament
in a by-election in 1967. He was the first member of
the CPS to be elected to the Parliament from a territorial constituency rather than the special constituencies
assigned at various times for graduates. He became involved in a constitutional crisis when Sadiq al-Mahdi
(q.v.) as Prime Minister worked to bar members of the
CPS from the Parliament. After the 1969 Revolution he
held a variety of cabinet posts, including Minister of
Economics (1969-70), of Industry (1970-1), and of Justice
(1971-2). He was known to be part of the nationalist

group within the CPS and disagreed with Abd al-Khaliq
Mahjub (q. v.).

SULAYMAN SOLONG. The first of the known historical rulers of the Keira (q. v.) dynasty in Darfur. He probably
reigned between 1640 and 1680 and is credited with the
formal introduction of state-supported Islam into Darfur.
Little is known of his actual life or rule, but he, his
son, and his grandson transformed their tribal kingdom
into a multi-ethnic successor state to the Tunjur (q. v.)
empire.

-T-

TABAQAT WAD DAYFALLAH. This is a biographical dictionary of Sudanese holy men compiled early in the 19th-cen-
tury by Muhammad al-Nur Wad Dayfallah (d. 1809). The
author was a Sudanese historian-jurist. The book is the
most important source for the religious and social history
of the Sudan during the Funj (q. v.) era. A partial translation into English appears in H. A. MacMichael's History of the Arabs in the Sudan.

TAFENG, EMIDIO. Southern soldier and political leader.
He was a commander in Anya Nya (q. v.). After the
breakup of the SSPG and its successor the Nile Provisional Government (q. v.), Tafeng announced the creation of the Anyidi Revolutionary Government (q. v.) because of the disunity among the civilian southern political leaders. The Anyidi Revolutionary Government was
soon absorbed by the South Sudan Liberation Movement
of Joseph Lagu (q. v.).

TAHA, MAHMUD MUHAMMAD see REPUBLICAN PARTY

TAHARQA. A Pharoah in the Kushite 25th Dynasty in Egypt
and a grandson of Kashta (q. v.), king of Kush. He fought
long wars against the Assyrians and was eventually driven
south. He ruled from 688 to 663 B. C.

TAHIR AL-MAJDHUB, al- see MAJDHUBIYYAH

TAJ AL-DIN AL-BAHARI see QADIRIYYAH

TAMBURA, d. 1913. A major chief of the Azande (q. v.).
He was captured in the 1870's by slave traders when his

father was killed in a battle between the Azande and the
forces of the slavers. He served in the Egyptian Army
and then was rewarded by being sent back to his home
country with arms. He fought Mahdist forces and established a broad area under his control in southwestern
Sudan. He recognized the superiority of European technology and cooperated with the French and then the British. This served to strengthen his own position in his
kingdom. He was succeeded by his son Renzi.

TANQASI CULTURE. A post-Meroitic culture, located between Dongola and Sennar. It is contemporary with the
Ballana Culture (q. v.) but more primitive. Some of its
pottery may be ancestral to later pottery in Alwa (q. v.).

TARIQAH. The Arabic word for "path" or "way." In Islamic society a tariqah is a set of devotional exercises established by a respected Sufi or mystic. The term is
also used for the organization, order, or brotherhood of
followers of such a respected Sufi teacher.

TAYYIB, ABDALLAH, al-, 1921-   . Sudanese intellectual
and writer. He studied at Gordon College and the University of London. He became professor of Arabic in
the University of Khartoum (1956), and then was Dean
of the Faculty of Arts. He is the author of many historical and literary studies as well as being a well-known
poet. In the 1970's he has served as Vice Chancellor
of the University of Khartoum.

THREE TOWNS. The large urban concentration at the confluence of the Blue and White Niles. The "towns" are
Omdurman, Khartoum, and Khartoum North.

TOM, al-. A leading family of the Kababish (q. v.).

TOM, ALI, al-, 1874-1938. The principle shaykh or nazir
of the Kababish (q. v.). He was one of the most influential tribal notables in the Condominium (q. v.) era. The
British policy of indirect rule helped him to unify the
tribe under his control. His family continues to have
influence in local and national politics.

TRIAD. A Saudi Arabian-based company with substantial
investments in Sudanese agricultural and industrial development.

TUNJUR. An early dynasty ruling in Darfur, replacing the
    Daju (q. v.). For a time Tunjur control may have ex-
    tended over Kanem and Wadai as well as Darfur. Their
    origins are obscure, with scholars suggesting the possi-
    bilities of north Africa or Christian Nubia. The state
    had some early connections with Islam. The traditional
    account of the end of the dynasty involves the historically
    obscure figure of Ahmad al-Ma'qur (q. v.), who provided
    a link with the subsequent Keira (q. v.) dynasty. The end
    of Tunjur rule came between 1580 and 1660.

TURABI, HASAN, al- see MUSLIM BROTHERHOOD

TURCO-EGYPTIAN REGIME. The government in the Sudan
    from 1821-1881. It was Egyptian in the sense that the
    Sudan was ruled by the governor of Egypt and it was
    Turkish in the sense that Egypt itself was still formally
    a part of the Ottoman (Turkish) Empire. Personnel in
    the government included people of Turkish, Egyptian, or
    more general Ottoman origin.

TURKIYYAH. The name given to the Turco-Egyptian regime
    (q. v.) ruling the Sudan from 1821-1881. In popular usage,
    the term has at times been used for any foreign regime
    in the modern era.

-U-

UBAYD HAJJ AL-AMIN, d. 1932. A Sudanese nationalist
    leader. He was a founder of the Sudan Union Society
    (q. v.) and then the White Flag League (q. v.). He work-
    ed in government departments but was dismissed and then
    imprisoned for his role in the 1924 nationalist uprisings.
    He died in jail.

ULAMA (also ULEMA). Muslim learned men, especially in
    knowledge of religious, primarily legal, matters.

UMARA DUNQAS see AMARA DUNQAS

UMMA PARTY. The Ansar-supported political party. It
    was formed in 1945 in reaction to the emergence of more
    radical political groups like the Ahigga (q. v.). Abd al-
    Rahman al-Mahdi (q. v.) gave the party his patronage and
    support. The Umma advocated a separate, independent
    Sudan and was always associated with Ansar interests.

Its president was Siddiq b. Abd al-Rahman al-Mahdi until his death in 1961. The party won 23 out of 97 seats
in the 1953 parliamentary elections and became the major opposition party. After independence it formed a coalition with the Peoples Democratic Party (q.v.) and Abdallah Khalil (q.v.) of the Umma became Prime Minister
(1956-8). The Umma won 63 out of 173 seats in the 1958
elections and remained the senior member of the ruling
coalition. This government was overthrown in 1958 by
the coup of Ibrahim Abboud (q.v.), and all parties were
outlawed. The Umma reemerged after the 1964 Revolution under the leadership of Sadiq al-Mahdi (q.v.), and
won 76 out of 173 seats in the 1965 elections. The party
allied itself with Ismail al-Azhari (q.v.) to form the government. In 1966-9 the party was split by a clash between Sadiq and the Ansar religious leader, al-Hadi al-
Mahdi. (See al-Mahdi family.) In coalition with al-
Azhari and the NUP (q.v.) the party provided the Sudan's
prime ministers (Muhammad Ahmad Mahjub, 1965-6 and
1967-9, and Sadiq al-Mahdi, 1966-7) until the 1969 Revolution brought an end to party politics.

UNIONIST PARTY (al-Ittihadiyyun). A small but influential
party formed in 1944. Leaders of the party, Hamad
Tawfiq Hamad (q.v.) and Khidr Hamad (q.v.), were well-
known intellectuals who had been active in the Abu Ra'uf
(q.v.) literary group in the 1930's and had been leaders
in the Graduates Congress (q.v.). The leaders continued
to be active in politics after the party was dissolved by
participating in the creation of the NUP (q.v.) in 1952.
The Unionists supported unity with Egypt on the basis of
dominion status for the Sudan. The leaders also hoped
to avoid the involvement of religious organizations in
politics although some had close ties with the Khatmiyyah
(q.v.).

UNITED FRONT FOR SUDANESE LIBERATION. A group
coordinating the efforts of pro-unity parties (except for
the National Front), Communist groups, students and
tenants associations, and the SWTUF (q.v.) for a brief
period in 1951-2. The association demanded immediate
termination of the Condominium (q.v.) government and
a United Nations plebiscite for Sudanese self-determination, and refused any cooperation with the British. The
United Front soon broke up and its constituents joined
other coalitions ranging from the NUP (q.v.) to the Anti-
Imperialist Front (q.v.).

UNITED FRONT FOR THE LIBERATION OF THE AFRICAN
SUDAN   see   GABOUSH, PHILLIP ABBAS

UNITY OF THE NILE VALLEY PARTY.   A smaller political
party formed in 1946 advocating the complete integration
of Egypt and the Sudan.   Its leader was Dardiri Ahmad
Ismail.   The party dissolved when it participated in the
creation of the NUP (q. v.) in 1952.

UTHMAN DIQNA, 1840-1926.   Mahdist commander in the eastern Sudan.   He came from a mercantile family in Suakin.
Romantic rumor said he was a Frenchman but his family
was probably of Kurdish origin.   Imprisoned for slave
trading, he opposed the Turco-Egyptian regime and was
converted to Mahdism very early.   He had been a disciple of al-Tahir al-Majdhub of the Majdhubiyyah (q. v.) but
he convinced his teacher to join the Mahdist cause.   Uthman was the commander in the east for both the Mahdi
and the Khalifah, Abdallahi al-Ta'ishi (q. v.), success-
fully leading Beja (q. v.) tribesmen against Egyptian and
British forces.   His troops were the "Fuzzy-Wuzzies"
made famous in the West by Kipling.   He remained the
key coordinator of Mahdist rule in the east but was forced
out of his primary camp by the British in 1891 and he
was no longer a major power.   He participated in the
battles of the Anglo-Egyptian conquest in 1898 and, in
1900, was the last leading Mahdist to be captured.   He
spent the rest of his life in prison or under close control, dying in Wadi Halfa.

-V-W-

VERONA FATHERS   see   COMBONI, DANIELE

W-GROUP.   A name given by early 20th-century archeologists,
and not widely used later, to the Greco-Roman remains
in Nubia from the Ptolemaic period.

WAD.   In Sudanese Arabic this means "son of..."   Thus,
"Wad Ahmad" means "son of Ahmad."

WAD AJIB.   Literally means "son of Ajib" and refers to the
descendants of Ajib, the son of Abdallah Jammā' (q. v.),
who held the title of "manjil" (q. v.) in the Funj (q. v.)
sultanate.

WAD AL-NUJUMI see ABD AL-RAHMAN WAD AL-NUJUMI

WAD DAYFALLAH see TABAQAT WAD DAYFALLAH

WAD HABUBA see ABD AL-QADIR WAD HABUBA

WAHHABI. The Wahhabi movement was a Muslim fundamentalist organization established in Arabia in the 18th-cen-
tury. It forms the basis for the leadership of the present kingdom of Saudi Arabia. Its reformist and puritan-
ical teachings have had widespread influence in the Islamic world.

WAWAT. An independent Nubian state in the 3rd millennium
B. C. The people of Wawat were probably of the C-
Group (q. v.).

WHITE FLAG LEAGUE. A nationalist organization founded
in 1924 by Ali Abd al-Latif (q. v.) and Ubayd Hajj al-
Amin (q. v.). It advocated unity with Egypt and drew
support from younger educated Sudanese. It was an important factor in the nationalist unrest and demonstrations in 1924. The leaders were jailed and the organization dissolved in the suppression of nationalism following 1924.

WINGATE, F. REGINALD, 1861-1953. British administrator
and soldier. He was a British soldier attached to the
Egyptian Army in 1884. He served actively in military
intelligence during the Mahdist period and was influential
in the development of British policy regarding the Sudan
and, through his writings, helped to shape the popular
British view of the Mahdiyyah. He served as governor-
general of the Sudan from 1899-1916 and was the principal architect of the actual structure of administration in
the Sudan under British rule. He served as High Commissioner in Egypt (1917-19) and then retired from public
life.

WOL WOL, LAWRENCE. Southern Sudanese political leader
of Dinka origin. He studied and received advanced de-
grees in Germany and France and then became active in
a series of southern organizations. He was an officer
in SANU (q. v.) and then acted as European representative of the Southern Sudan Liberation Movement of Joseph
Lagu (q. v.) and earlier Nile Provisional Government
(q. v.). For a time he was editor of Voice of the South-

ern Sudan (London). He participated in the negotiations
leading up to the Addis Ababa Agreement of 1972 (q. v.).
After the settlement he was named Minister of State for
Planning and then Minister of Planning in the Sudanese
government. He was elected to the Southern Regional
Peoples Assembly in 1973 and has served in the southern
High Executive Committee. In 1976 he was named Sudan-
ese ambassador to Uganda.

WORKERS FORCE. A political group formed in 1967. It
was led by radical union leaders, especially from the
Sudan Railway Workers. It won one seat in the parliamentary elections of 1968 in the railroad center of Atbara.

-X-Y-

X-GROUP. The culture and population of Lower Nubia which
flourished in the A. D. 200's to 500's. It was a post-
Meroitic mixture of Roman-Byzantine, Kushite, and new
elements creating a distinctive culture. In origin some
scholars believe the X-Group people to be new migrants
into the region while others stress the continuity of development from earlier groups. The Ballana Culture
(q. v.) is believed to be X-Group and most authorities
identify the X-Group with Nobatia (q. v.).

Y-GROUP. A name given by early 20th-century archeologists,
and not widely used later, for the Nubian Christian remains of the 6th through 12th centuries.

YAM. An independent trading kingdom in the 3rd millennium
B. C. , probably centered in the Kerma area. It may have
been the prototype for the later Kerma Culture (q. v.).

YAMBIO, d. 1905. A major chief of the Azande (q. v.). He
assumed control over his father's kingdom in the 1860's.
He was hostile to newcomers and fought the Egyptian government, slave traders, and other Zande princes. This
tradition continued with wars against the Mahdists, and,
finally, against the British. After a number of battles,
he was defeated in 1905 and died soon after.

YA'QUBĀB. A major religious family with branches in the
Sennar and Shendi areas. The founder, Muhammad ibn
Hamad Ban al-Naqa (ca. 1550) was an early leader of the

Qadiriyyah (q. v.) in the Sudan. Salih Ban al-Naqa
(1681-1753) established the Shendi branch and had religious prestige in the northern Funj (q. v.) areas, as
did his son, Abd al-Rahman (born 1709). The Ya'qubab
affliated with the Sammaniyyah (q. v.) around 1800 under
the leadership of Shaykh al-Tum Ban al-Naqa. The line
of khalifahs (q. v.) of the Ya'qubab was interrupted briefly
during the Mahdist times but was reestablished in the
20th-century.

-Z-

ZANDE. Singular of Azande (q. v.).

ZANDE SCHEME. A major development effort in southwestern Sudan begun after World War II. It was an attempt
to create a largescale agricultural scheme and processing
industry to aid the Azande (q. v.). Transportation and
other costs as well as the growing civil war in the south
brought much of the operation to an end.

ZARRUQ, HASAN AL-TAHIR, 1916- . Sudanese political
leader and teacher. He was educated at Gordon College,
graduating from the teachers section in 1935. He taught
in a variety of schools until he was dismissed from government service in 1948 for political activities. He was
a founder of the Liberal Party (q. v.) in 1944, leading
the Liberal Unionist section that favored unity with Egypt.
He was active in party alliances after World War II,
helping to lead opposition to the Legislative Assembly
(q. v.) and serving as assistant secretary to the United
Front for Sudanese Liberation (q. v.). Rather than joining the NUP (q. v.) he was one of the founders of the
Anti-Imperialist Front (q. v.) in 1953 and was elected to
Parliament in that year. He was increasingly associated
publically with the Communist Party of the Sudan and was
editor of al-Midan, a communist newspaper in Khartoum.
He was elected to Parliament in 1965 from the special
graduates constituency.

ZARRUQ, MUBARAK, 1916-1965. Sudanese political leader.
He graduated from Gordon College and was active in
early nationalist and intellectual organizations. He was
on the executive committee of the first Students Union
in 1940 and was active in the activities of the Graduates
Congress (q. v.). He worked with the Sudan Railways

(1934-9) and then entered law school, setting up practice
as an advocate in 1943. He served on the executive
committee of the Graduates Congress and of the Ashigga
Party (q. v.). He was a close friend and associate of
Ismail al-Azhari (q. v.). After World War II he was active in a number of organizations, being elected to the
Omdurman Municipal Council (1950), and acting as secretary of the United Front for Sudanese Liberation (q. v.).
He became a member of the NUP when it was created
in 1952 and was elected to Parliament in 1953. He was
named Minister of Communications in al-Azhari's first
cabinet and joined al-Azhari in opposition after 1956.
He took part in the 1964 Revolution and was Minister of
Finance in the transition government (1964-5) but he died
suddenly just before the 1965 elections.

ZUBAYR PASHA RAHMA MANSUR, 1830-1913. Slave trader
and adventurer. He was from a branch of the Jaaliyyin
(q. v.) and established himself as a major commercial
and military force in the southern Sudan. By 1865 with
his private army he was the virtual ruler of Bahr al-
Ghazal and in 1874 he conquered much of Darfur. The
Turco-Egyptian governors mistrusted him although he
officially cooperated with them. After 1875 he was detained in Cairo. He was suggested as a leader who might
be sent to the Sudan to fight the Mahdi but this project
was not carried out. In 1899 the new governor-general,
F. R. Wingate (q. v.), secured his return to the Sudan
where he functioned as a counselor to the new government and maintained a large farm.

BIBLIOGRAPHY

Table of Contents

Introduction

A wide variety of information on the Sudan is available to the reader of English. Both Sudanese and Western scholars have written valuable works analyzing and interpreting the history and culture of the Sudan. It is thus possible to learn about major aspects of the Sudanese experience from a variety of perspectives.

General reference works of special value are Richard Hill, A Biographical Dictionary of the Sudan, which covers from ancient times to the 20th century; Mandour el-Mahdi, A Short History of the Sudan, which presents a summary of Sudanese history from antiquity to present times; and two general, multidisciplinary descriptions are H. D. Nelson, Area Handbook for the Democratic Republic of the Sudan, published by the U. S. Government Printing Office, and Sudan Today, prepared by the Sudanese Ministry of Information and Culture.

The ancient and medieval periods of Sudanese history are exciting areas of new studies. The many archeological projects of the past few years are opening new vistas of history and new books and studies are constantly appearing. One book that tries to draw much of the new information together is William Y. Adams, Nubia, Corridor to Africa.

Publications of the Sudanese Antiquities Service and the journal Kush are a source of new information. Valuable summary studies in this area include P. L. Shinnie, Meroe, A
Civilization of the Sudan and Fritz and Ursala Hintze, Civilizations of the Old Sudan, which is a short, readable, and
well-illustrated book.

For the pre-modern Islamic era, two relatively new
works are very useful. They are Yusuf Fadl Hasan, The
Arabs and the Sudan, from the Seventh to the Early Sixteenth
Century, and R. S. O'Fahey and J. L. Spaulding, Kingdoms
of the Sudan. An older but still useful reference work is
H. A. MacMichael, A History of the Arabs in the Sudan.

For the modern era a variety of sources are available.
A helpful general introduction is P. M. Holt, A Modern History of the Sudan. Richard Hill, Egypt in the Sudan, 1820-
1881 gives an account of the Turco-Egyptian period and P.
M. Holt, The Mahdist State in the Sudan, 1881-1898, is the
standard work on the Mahdist period. The latter can be sup-
plemented with the readable, often exciting literature of "the
prisoners of the Mahdi" type, like Rudolf von Slatin, Fire
and Sword in the Sudan. However, it should be remembered
that much of this material originated as anti-Mahdist war
propaganda. Many of the same biases appear in the writings
about Charles "Chinese" Gordon. For an insider's view of
the Mahdiyyah, one can read The Memoirs of Babikr Bedri.

A variety of perspectives is now available on the history of the Anglo-Egyptian period (1899-1956). Many British
administrators wrote accounts of their experiences, as in
H. C. Jackson, Sudan Days and Ways, and others wrote more
general accounts. One of the more interesting was written
by a former Civil Secretary, H. A. MacMichael, called The
Sudan, and another account centered around the life of another
Civil Secretary: The Making of the Modern Sudan: The Life
and Letters of Sir Douglas Newbold, by K. D. D. Henderson.
For Sudanese perspectives, one should read the scholarly accounts in M. Abd al-Rahim, Imperialism and Nationalism in
the Sudan and M. O. Beshir, Revolution and Nationalism in
the Sudan.

A good overview of Sudanese political development
since independence is provided by Peter Bechtold in Politics
in the Sudan. An issue of the history of the independent Sudan that has received much attention is the "Southern Problem." An excellent brief summary of both the southern con-

flict and southern history can be found in Robert O. Collins, The Southern Sudan in Historical Perspective. A southern view, written before the settlement of 1972, is O. Albino, The Sudan, A Southern Viewpoint. A more comprehensive coverage is provided in the two books by the northern Sudanese writer, M. O. Beshir, The Southern Sudan: Background to Conflict and The Southern Sudan: From Conflict to Peace.

In social and cultural analysis, the richest area is anthropology. Many of the now classical tribal studies were done in the Sudan. The best known are the works of E. E. Evans-Pritchard (e. g. , The Nuer, Witchcraft, Oracles, and Magic Among the Azande). Recent studies of the Dinka by Francis Deng, especially Tradition and Modernization: A Challenge for Law among the Dinka of the Sudan, are already well known. While earlier studies tended to concentrate on southern tribes, studies of northern groups have now become more common. Some of the best of these are Talal Asad, The Kababish Arabs, and Ian Cunnison, Baggara Arabs.

Other fields may not be as rich in variety or depth but still have good coverage. In economics there are valuable special studies like J. D. Tothill, Agriculture in the Sudan; A. Gaitskell, Gezira, A Story of Development in the Sudan; Sa'd al-Din Fawzi, The Labour Movement in the Sudan, 1946-1955; and Mohamed Abdel Rahman Ali, Government Expenditure and Economic Development, A Case Study of the Sudan. In religion, no general survey of Sudanese Islam has appeared in English since the now-dated but still helpful Islam in the Sudan by J. S. Trimingham. The standard reference in geographical studies is K. M. Barbour, The Republic of the Sudan: A Regional Geography.

To follow current affairs in the Sudan, people can use the biweekly chronology, Arab Report and Record, published in London, or the chronology section of the Middle East Journal, published in Washington by the Middle East Institute. In the latter, the lists of recently published books and articles provide a means for updating bibliographies. The annual reviews in Africa Contemporary Record are also helpful.

GENERAL

REFERENCE, INFORMATION, GENERAL HISTORY

Adams, William Y. Nubia: Corridor to Africa. Princeton, N. J. : Princeton University Press, 1976.

Africa Contemporary Record, Annual Survey and Documents. London: Rex Collings. Published annually, beginning in 1968.

American Universities Field Staff. Northeast Africa Series-- Reports Service, 2. Sudan--Collected Works. (Bound volumes and continuing series.)

Bosayli, al-Sh. An Outline History of the Sudan Nile Valley. Cairo: Arab Bookshop, 1966.

Collins, Robert O., and Tignor, Robert L. Egypt and the Sudan. Englewood Cliffs, N.J.: Prentice-Hall, 1967.

Cookson, John A., et al. Area Handbook for the Republic of the Sudan, 2nd ed. Washington: U.S. Gov. Printing Office, 1964.

Gleichen, A., ed. The Anglo-Egyptian Sudan: A Compendium Prepared by Officers of the Sudan Government. London: H.M.S.O., 1905. 2 vols.

Hamilton, J. A. de C., ed. The Anglo-Egyptian Sudan from Within. London: Faber & Faber, 1935.

Hasan, Yusuf Fadl., ed. Sudan in Africa. Khartoum: Khartoum University Press, 1971.

Henderson, K. D. D. Sudan Republic. New York: Praeger, 1965.

Hill, Richard. A Biographical Dictionary of the Sudan, 2nd ed. London: Cass, 1967.

_____. Sudan Transport: A History of Railway, Marine and River Services in the Republic of the Sudan. London: Oxford University Press, 1965.

Holt, Peter M. A Modern History of the Sudan; From the Funj Sultanate to the Present Day. New York: Grove Press, 1961.

_____. "The Nilotic Sudan," in The Cambridge History of Islam, P. M. Holt, A. K. S. Lambton, and B. Lewis, eds. Cambridge, England: Cambridge University Press, 1970; vol 2, pp. 327-344.

Krotki, Karol J. Twenty-One Facts about the Sudanese. Khartoum: Ministry of Social Affairs, 1958.

MacMichael, H. A. A History of the Arabs in the Sudan.
New York: Barnes and Noble, 1967 (reprint of 1922 ed.).
2 vols.

Mahdi, Mandour, el-. A Short History of the Sudan. London: Oxford University Press, 1965.

Middle East and North Africa. London: Europa Publications.
Annually published as a reference work, beginning in
1948. 1976-1977 is the 23rd ed.

Moorehead, Alan. The Blue Nile. New York: Harper, 1972.

_____. The White Nile, 2nd ed. New York: Harper, 1971.

Nelson, Harold D., et al. Area Handbook for the Democratic Republic of the Sudan. Washington: U.S. Gov. Printing Office, 1973.

Randell, J. "Sudan," Focus, vol. 17, no. 1 (Sept. 1966),
1-6.

"Republic of the Sudan," Department of State Background
Notes. Washington: Department of State and U.S. Gov.
Printing Office, 1971.

Sandwith, F. M. "Egypt and the Egyptian Sudan (1841-1907),"
in The Cambridge Modern History, A. W. Ward, G. W.
Prothero, and S. Leathes, eds. Cambridge, England:
Cambridge University Press, 1910; vol. 12, pp. 429-456
in the 1934 reprinted ed.

Sudan. External Information and International Relations Administration. Facts About the Sudan. Khartoum: Republic of the Sudan, n.d.

_____. Ministry of Information and Culture (Sudan). Sudan
Today. Nairobi: University Press of Africa, 1971.

Trigger, Bruce. "The Personality of the Sudan," in Eastern
African History, D. F. McCall, N. R. Bennett, and
J. Butler, eds. New York: Praeger, 1969; III, 74-99.

TRAVEL AND DESCRIPTION

Baker, Anne. Morning Star: Florence Baker's Diary of the

Expedition to Put Down the Slave Trade on the Nile,
1870-1873. London: Kimber, 1972.

Baker, Samuel White. The Albert N'Yanza: Great Basin of
the Nile and Explorations of the Nile Sources. Detroit:
Negro Universities Press, 1970 (reprint of 1869 ed.).

_____. Exploration of the Nile Tributaries of Abysinnia.
Hartford, Conn.: Case, 1868.

_____. In the Heart of Africa. Westport, Conn.: Negro
Universities Press, 1970 (reprint).

_____. Ismailia. New York: Negro Universities Press,
1969 (reprint of 1874 two-vol. ed.).

_____. The Nile Tributaries of Abysinnia and the Sword
Hunters of the Hamran Arabs. New York: Johnson
Reprint Corp., 1971 (reprint of 1867 ed.).

Bernatzik, H. A. Gari-Gari: The Call of the African Wil-
derness. London: Constable, 1939.

Beveridge, Charles E. G. Allah Laughed. Melbourne:
National Press, 1950.

Blashford-Snell, J. et al. "Conquest of the Blue Nile,"
Geographical Journal, vol. 136, pt. 1 (March 1970),
42-60.

Bourchier, Capt. W. Narrative of a Passage from Bombay
to England. London: Whittaker, 1834.

Brander, Bruce, The River Nile. Washington: National
Geographic Society, 1966.

Brockway, A. F. African Journey. London: Gollancz, 1955.

Budge, Ernest Alfred. The Nile. Westport, Conn.: Negro
Universities Press, 1970 (reprint of 1912 ed.).

Dugmore, A. Radclyffe. Through the Sudan. (Pitman's
Travel Series.) London: Pitman, 1938.

_____. The Vast Sudan. London: Arrowsmith, 1924.

Edwards, Amelia B. A Thousand Miles Up the Nile, 2nd ed.

New York: Burt, 1888.

Elisofon, Eliot. The Nile. London: Cape, 1964.

Hill, R. L. "The Search for the White Nile's Source: Two Explorers Who Failed," Geographical Journal, 1956, pp. 247-50.

Hoogstraal, H. "South in the Sudan," National Geographic Magazine, vol. 103 (1953), 249-72.

Hoskins, G. A. Travels in Ethiopia. London: Longman, Rees, 1835.

Hurst, H. E. The Nile. London: Constable, 1952.

Ibrahim al-Adawi. "Description of the Sudan by Muslim Geographers and Travellers," Sudan Notes and Records, vol. 35 (1954), 5-16.

James, Frank. The Wild Tribes of the Soudan. New York: Negro Universities Press, 1969 (reprint of 1883 ed.).

Johnston, H. The Nile Quest. London: Lawrence and Bullen, 1903.

Junker, Wilhelm. Travels in Africa During the Years 1875-1878, trans. A. H. Keane. London: Chapman and Hall, 1890.

_____. Travels in Africa During the Years 1879-1883, trans. A. H. Keane. London: Chapman and Hall, 1891.

Kinross, Lord. "The Nile," Horizon, vol. 8, no. 3 (1966), 80-99.

Langley, Michael. No Woman's Country: Travels in the Anglo-Egyptian Sudan. London: Jarrolds, 1950.

Lepsius, C. R. Discoveries in Egypt, Ethiopia and the Peninsula of Sinai, 2nd ed. London: Bentley, 1852.

_____. Letters from Egypt, Ethiopia, and the Peninsula of Sinai, trans. Leonora and Joanna B. Horner. London: Bohn, 1853.

Mann, Anthony. Where God Laughed. London: Museum Press, 1954.

Page, Thomas N.   On the Nile in 1901.   Coconut Grove,
    Fla. :   Field Research Papers, n. d.

Pallme, Ignatius.   Travels in Kordofan.   London: Madden,
    1844.

Parry, E. G.   Suakin, 1885, 2nd ed.   London: Kegan Paul
    Trench, 1886.

Percy, A. P. Baron Prudhoe.   "Extracts from Private
    Memoranda Kept by Lord Prudhoe on a Journey from
    Cairo to Sennar, in 1829, Describing the Peninsula of
    Sennar," Journal of the Royal Geographical Society,
    vol. 5 (1835), 38-59.

Petherick, John.   Travels in Central Africa and Explorations
    of the Western Nile Tributaries.   Farnborough: Gregg,
    1968 (reprint of 1869 ed.).

Plowden, Walter Chichele.   Travels in Abyssinia.   London:
    Longmans, Green, 1868.

St. John, James August.   Egypt and Mohammed Ali; or,
    Travels in the Valley of the Nile.   London, 1834.

Speke, John H.   What Led to the Discovery of the Source
    of the Nile.   London: Cass, 1967 (reprint of 1864 ed.).

Taylor, Bayard.   A Journey to Central Africa; or, Life and
    Landscapes from Egypt to the Negro Kingdoms of the
    White Nile.   New York: Negro Universities Press, 1970
    (reprint of 1854 ed.).

Tothill, B.   "An Expedition in Central Africa by Three Dutch
    Ladies," Sudan Notes and Records, vol. 28 (1947), 25-49.

Ward, John.   Our Sudan, Its Pyramids and Progress.   Lon-
    don: Murray, 1905.

BIBLIOGRAPHIES

Andrew, G.   Sources of Information on the Geology of the
    Anglo-Egyptian Sudan.   Khartoum: Geological Survey
    Department Bulletin 3, 1945.

Bayoumi, A. A.   Forest Bibliography of the Sudan up to 1973.
    Khartoum: National Council for Research, 1974.

Collins, Robert O. "Egypt and the Sudan," in The Historio-
graphy of the British Empire--Commonwealth Trends,
Interpretations and Resources, ed. R. W. Winks. Durham, N. C.: Duke University Press, 1961; pp. 281-91.

Dagher, Joseph Assaad. Sudanese Bibliography, Arabic
Sources (1875-1967). Beirut: Librairie Orientale, 1968.

Evans-Pritchard, E. E. "Bibliographical Note on the Ethnology of the Southern Sudan," Africa, (1940), 62-67.

_____. "Sources, with Particular Reference to the Southern
Sudan," Cahiers d'Etudes Afrique, vol. 11, no. 41
(1971), 129-79.

Gadallah, Fawzi. "Meroitic Problems and a Comprehensive
Meroitic Bibliography," Kush, vol. 11 (1963), 196-216.

Geddes, C. L. An Analytical Guide to the Bibliographies on
Modern Egypt and the Sudan. Denver: American Institute of Islamic Studies, 1972.

Hill, Richard L. A Bibliography of the Anglo-Egyptian Sudan, from the Earliest Times to 1937. Oxford: Oxford
University Press, 1939.

_____. "The Gordon Literature," Durham University Jour-
nal, vol. 47 (1955), 97-103.

_____. "Historical Writing on the Sudan Since 1820," in
Historians of the Middle East, B. Lewis and P. M. Holt,
eds. London: Oxford University Press, 1962; pp. 357-66.

Holt, P. M. "The Source Materials of the Sudanese Mahdiya," St. Antony's Papers No. 4: Middle Eastern Affairs, No. 1. London: Chatto & Windus, 1958.

McClanahan, Grant V. "Postwar Books on the Anglo-Egyptian
Sudan," Middle East Journal, vol. 6 (1952), 341-46.

McLoughlin, P. F. Research for Agricultural Development
in Northern Sudan to 1967: A Classified Inventory and
Analysis. Frederickton, N. B.: McLoughlin Associates,
1971.

Nasri, Abdel Rahman, el-. A Bibliography of the Sudan,
1938-1958. London: Oxford University Press, 1962.

Sanderson, G. N. "The Modern Sudan, 1820-1956: The
    Present Position of Historical Studies," Journal of Afri-
    can History, vol. 4 (1963), 432-61.

Struck, B. "A Bibliography of the Languages of the Southern
    Sudan," Sudan Notes and Records, vol. 11 (1928).

Theses on the Sudan, 2nd ed. Khartoum: University of
    Khartoum Library, 1971.

AUDIO-VISUAL INFORMATION

"Action Sudan: The Church and the Peace" (motion picture).
    Interchurch Committee for World Development and Re-
    lief, Canada, and Church World Service, 1974. (Made
    by Religious Television Associates, Toronto.)

"The Forgotten Kingdom" (motion picture). BBC-TV, London,
    1971. Released in the United States by Time-Life Films.

"Khartoum" (motion picture). Julian Blaustein Productions,
    England, 1966. Released in the United States by United
    Artists Corporation.

"Nile Basin, Part 2: Sudan" (filmstrip). Hulton Press,
    London, 195?.

"Republic of Sudan" (filmstrip). Eye Gate House, London,
    1962.

"The Wealth of the Sudan" (filmstrip). Hulton Press, Lon-
    don, 195?.

FOR YOUNGER READERS

Drower, Margaret. Nubia: A Drowning Land. London:
    Longmans, 1970.

Griffiths, V. L. Khartoum. (Tropical Library: Cities of
    the World.) London: Longmans, 1958.

Henderson, Larry. Egypt and the Sudan: Countries of the
    Nile. New York: Nelson, 1971.

Hodgkin, Robin A. How People Live in the Sudan. London:

Educational Supply Assoc., 1963.

Hyslop, John. <u>Sudan Story</u>. London: Naldrett Press, 1952.

<u>Sudan</u>, in <u>Enchantment of Africa Series</u>, ed. Allan Carpenter. Chicago: Children's Press, 1972- .

CULTURAL

ARCHITECTURE AND ARTS

Delmege, J. de G. "Art in the Southern Sudan," <u>Sudan Notes and Records</u>, vol. 3 (1920).

Hale, Sandra. "Arts in a Changing Society: Northern Sudan," <u>Ufamo</u> (Khartoum), vol. 1, no. 11 (1970), 64-79.

_____. "Sudanese Cultural Renaissance: Social Themes Have Brought About a Flowering of Written, Sung, and Spoken Word," <u>Africa Report</u>, vol. 15, no. 9 (Dec. 1970), 29-31.

Jungraithmayr, Herrmann. "Rock Paintings in the Sudan," <u>Current Anthropology</u>, vol. 2, no. 4 (Oct. 1961), 388-9.

Kronenberg, Andreas. "Wooden Carvings in the South Western Sudan," <u>Kush</u>, vol. 8 (1960), 274-281.

Lee, D. "Factors Influencing Choice of House Type: A Geographic Analysis from the Sudan," <u>Professional Geographer</u>, vol. 21, no. 6 (Nov. 1969, 393-7.

_____. "Mud Mansions of Northern Sudan," <u>African Arts</u>, (1971-2), 60-62.

_____. "Mud Mansions of Northern Sudan," <u>Ekistics</u>, vol. 38 (Oct. 1974), 244-6.

_____. "The Nubian House: Persistence of a Cultural Tradition," <u>Landscape</u>, vol. 18, no. 1 (1969), 36-9.

Nur, Sadiq, al-. "Origin and Development of Conical Straw Huts in the Sudan," <u>Antiquity</u>, (1953), pp. 240-2.

Olderogge, Dmitry, and Forman, Werner. The Art of
   Africa: Negro Art from the Institute of Ethnography,
   Leningrad. New York: Hamlyn, 1969.

"Painter From the Sudan: El Salahi," African Arts, vol. 1,
   no. 1 (1967), 16-26.

Wenzel, Marian. House Decoration in Nubia. London:
   Duckworth, 1972.

Witherspoon, L. M. "Some Paintings by Art Students of the
   Sudan at the Omdurman Training College," Studio,
   no. 137 (1949), 118-9.

SUDANESE LANGUAGES, LITERATURE, LINGUISTICS

Abbas, Ali Abdalla. "Notes of Tayeb Salih: Season of Migration to the North and The Wedding of Zein," Sudan
   Notes and Records, vol. 55 (1974), 46-60.

Abdalla, Abdelgadir M. "A System for the Dissection of
   Meroitic Complexes," Sudan Notes and Records, vol. 54
   (1973), 81-93.

Armbruster, Charles H. Dongolese Nubian: Lexicon.
   New York: Cambridge University Press, 1965.

Bell, Herman. "An Extinct Nubian Language from Kordofan,"
   Sudan Notes and Records, vol. 54 (1973), 73-80.

_____. "The Tone System of Mahas Nubian," Journal of
   American Languages, vol. 7 (1968), 26-32.

Boullata, Issa J. "Encounter Between East and West: A
   Theme in Contemporary Arabic Novels," Middle East
   Journal, vol. 30, no. 1 (Winter 1976), 49-62.

Bryan, M. A. "A Linguistic No-man's Land," Africa,
   vol. 15 (1945), 188-205.

_____, and Tucker, A. N. Distribution of the Nilotic and
   Nilo-Hamitic Languages of Africa. London: Oxford
   University Press, 1948.

Crazzolara, J. P. A Study of the Acholi Language, Grammar,
   and Vocabulary. London: Oxford University Press, 1938.

Evans-Pritchard, E. E.   "Azande Slang Language," Man,
    vol. 54 (1954), 185-6.

_____ . "Sanza, a Characteristic Feature of Zande Language
    and Thought," Bulletin of The School of Oriental and
    African Studies (London), vol. 18 (1956), 161-80.

Greenberg, J. H.   "Nilotic, Nilo-Hamitic and Hamito-Semi-
    tic," Africa, vol. 27 (1957), 364-78.

_____ . Studies in African Linguistic Classification.   New
    Haven: Compass, 1955.

Hair, P.   "A Layman's Guide to the Languages of the Sudan
    Republic," Sudan Notes and Records, vol. 47 (1966),
    65-78.

Hillelson, S.   "Classical Reminiscences in Popular Litera-
    ture," Sudan Notes and Records, vol. 30 (1949), 271-2.

_____ . Sudan Arabic Texts.   Cambridge, England: Cam-
    bridge University Press, 1935.

Kohler, O.   "The Early Study of the Nilotic Languages of
    the Sudan," Sudan Notes and Records, vol. 51 (1970),
    85-94, and vol. 52 (1971), 56-62.

MacMillan, M.   Some Aspects of Bilingualism in University
    Education.   Khartoum: Sudan Research Unit, 1970.

Malander, A.   A New Acholi Grammar.   Nairobi: Eagle
    Press, 1954.

Nalder, Leonard F., ed.   A Tribal Survey of Mongalla Prov-
    ince.   New York: Negro Universities Press, 1970,
    (reprint of 1937 ed.).

Nebel, A.   Dinka Grammar.   Verona: Missioni Africane,
    1948.

Trigger, Bruce.   "Meroitic and Eastern Sudanic: A Linguis-
    tic Relationship?" Kush, vol. 12 (1964), 188-94.

Trimingham, J. S.   Sudan Colloquial Arabic.   London:
    Oxford University Press, 1946.

Tucker, A. N.   The Eastern Sudanic Languages.   London:
    Dawsons, 1967.

SUDAN RELATED FICTION IN ENGLISH

Atiyah, E. Black Vanguard. London: Davies, 1952.

Barry, Milo. Bondage: Dervishes in the Sudan. Van Nuys,
    Calif.: United Service, 1956.

Doyle, A. C. The Tragedy of the Korosko. 1898 and other
    editions.

Gartner, Chloe. Drums of Khartoum. New York: Morrow,
    1967.

Henriques, R. D. Q. No Arms, No Armour. London:
    Collins, 1951.

Kipling, R. The Light That Failed. London: Macmillan,
    1898.

Mason, A. E. W. The Four Feathers. 1902 and other
    editions.

Sawkins, J. Jangara. London: Longmans, 1963.

Tayeb Salih, Season of Migration to the North, trans. Denys
    Johnson-Davies. London: Heinemann Educational Books,
    1967.

_____. The Wedding of Zein and Other Stories, trans.
    Denys Johnson-Davies. London: Heinemann, 1968.

Wyndham, R. Gentle Savage. London: Cassell, 1938.

SCIENTIFIC

GEOGRAPHY

Ali, A. I. M. "A History of European Geographical Explor-
    ation of the Sudan, 1820-1865," Sudan Notes and Records,
    vol. 55 (1974), 1-15.

Barbour, K. M. "North and South in Sudan, A Study in
    Human Contrasts," Annals of the Association of Amer-
    ican Geographers, vol. 54, no. 2 (June 1964), 209-226.

_____. The Republic of the Sudan: A Regional Geography. London: University of London Press, 1961.

Berry, L. "Geographical Research in Sudan," Proceedings of the Twelfth Annual Conference of the Philosophical Society of Sudan, 1964.

_____, and Whiteman, A. J. "The Nile in the Sudan," Geographical Journal, vol. 134 (1968), 1-37.

Bushra, el-Sayed, el-. "The Development of Industry in Greater Khartoum, Sudan," The East African Geographical Review, no. 10 (April 1972), 27-50.

_____. "The Evolution of the Three Towns," African Urban Notes, vol. 6, no. 2 (Summer 1971), 8-23.

_____. "Occupational Classification of Sudanese Towns," Sudan Notes and Records, vol. 50 (1969), 75-96.

_____. "Regional Inequalities in the Sudan," Focus (American Geographical Society), vol. 26, no. 1 (Sept. -Oct. 1975), 1-8.

_____. "Towns in the Sudan in the Eighteenth and Early Nineteenth Centuries," Sudan Notes and Records, vol. 52 (1971), 63-70.

Doxiadis Associates, Land Use and Water Survey in Kordofan Province, Sudan Republic, Bulletin no. 71 (1964).

Hodgkin, R. A. Sudan Geography. London: Longmans, 1951.

Kuba, G. K. Climate of the Sudan. Khartoum: University of Khartoum, National Building Research Station, 1968.

Lebon, J. H. G. Land Use in Sudan. (Regional Monograph no. 4 in the World Land Use Survey, edited by Dudley Stamp.) Bude, Cornwall, England: Geographical Publications, 1965.

Roden, David. "Regional Inequality and Rebellion in the Sudan," Geographical Review, vol. 64, no. 4 (Oct. 1974), 498-516.

Sharaf, A. T. "A Geographical Assessment of Health Prob-

lems and Disease Incidence in the Sudan," Geographica
Medica, vol. 3 (1972), 30-106.

Tom, Mahdi Amin, el-. The Rains of the Sudan. Khartoum:
Khartoum University Press, 1975.

_____. "The Relative Dryness of the White Nile," Sudan
Notes and Records, vol. 55 (1974), 161-166.

_____. "Toward a Rational Estimation of Average Rainfall
in the Sudan," Sudan Notes and Records, vol. 53 (1972),
123-151.

GEOLOGY

Andrew, G. "Geology of the Sudan," in Tothill, J. D.
Agriculture in the Sudan. London: Oxford University
Press, 1948; pp. 84-128.

Blandford, W. T. Observations on the Geology and Zoology
of Abyssinia Made During the Progress of the British
Expedition to That Country in 1867-68. London, 1869.

Boushi, Ismail Mudathir, el-. "The Shallow Ground Water
of the Gezira Formation at Khartoum and the Northern
Gezira," Sudan Notes and Records, vol. 53 (1972),
152-61.

Cahen, L., and Snelling, N. J. The Geochronology of Equatorial Africa. North Holland, 1966.

Delany, F. M. "Recent Contributions to the Geology of the
Sudan," Nineteenth International Geological Congress,
Algiers. Vol. 20, 11-18.

Girdler, R. W. "Geophysical Studies of Rift Valleys," in
Ahrens, L. N., et al., Physics and Chemistry of the
Earth, vol. 5. New York: Pergamon Press, 1964.

_____. "The Relationship of the Red Sea to the East Afri-
can Rift System," Quarterly Journal of the Geological
Society of London, vol. 114 (1958), 79-105.

Heinzelin, J. de, and Paepe, R. "The Geological History
of the Nile Valley in Sudanese Nubia. Preliminary Results," in Contribution to the Prehistory of Nubia,

assembled by F. Wendorf. Dallas, Texas: Southern
Methodist University Press, 1964.

Kleinsorge, H., and Zscheked, J. G. Geologic and Hydro-
logic Research in the Arid and Semi-arid Zone of Western Sudan. Hanover: Amt für Bordenforschung, 1958.

Lofti, M., and Kabesh, M. L. "On a New Classification of
the Basement Complex Rocks of the Red Sea Hills, Sudan," Bulletin Soc. Geogr. Egypte, vol. 38 (1964),
91-99.

Mula, Hafiz G. "A Geophysical Survey of J. Aulia Region,"
Sudan Notes and Records, vol. 53 (1972), 162-166.

Sandford, K. S., and Arkell, W. J. "On the Relation of
Paleolithic Man to the History and Geology of the Nile
Valley in Egypt," Man, vol. 29 (1929), 65.

Swartz, D. H., and Arden, D. D., Jr. "Geological History
of the Red Sea Area," Bulletin of the American Association of Petroleum Geologists, vol. 44 (1960), 1621-37.

Whiteman, A. J. "Comments on the Classification of the
Basement Complex of the Red Sea Hills," Sudan Notes
and Records, vol. 51 (1970), 126-30.

_____. "Geological Research in the Sudan," Proceedings
of the Twelfth Annual Conference of the Philosophical
Society of Sudan, 1964, pp. 219-39.

_____. The Geology of the Sudan Republic. Oxford, Eng-
land: Clarendon Press, 1971.

Worral, G. A. "A Simple Introduction to the Geology of the
Sudan," Sudan Notes and Records, vol. 38 (1957), 2-9.

MEDICINE AND HEALTH

Ahmad Abd al-Halim. "Native Medicines in the Northern
Sudan," Sudan Notes and Records, vol. 22 (1939), 27-48.

Anis al-Shami. "Health Problems in the Sudan," El Hakeim
(Khartoum), vol. 1 (1957), 27-36.

Ayad, N. "Bilharziasis Survey in Somaliland, Eritrea,

Ethiopia, the Sudan and Yemen," Bulletin of the World
Health Organization, 1956, pp. 1-117.

Bloss, J. F. E. "Notes on the Health of the Sudan Prior
to the Present Government," Sudan Notes and Records,
vol. 24 (1941), 131-44.

Bousfield, L. Sudan Doctor. London: Johnson, 1954.

Cruickshank, Alexander. The Kindling Fire, Medical Adven-
tures in the Southern Sudan. London: Heinemann, 1962.

Erwa, Hashim H. , Satti, M. H. , and Abbas, A. M. "Cere-
brospinal Meningitis in the Sudan," Sudan Notes and Records, vol. 52 (1971), 101-109.

Food and Society in the Sudan. Proceedings of the Philosophical Society of the Sudan, 1953.

el-Hakeim. Journal published by the Students' Medical Society, University of Khartoum, beginning publication in
1957.

Hoogstraal, Harry H. and Heyneman, Donald. "Leishmania-
sis in the Sudan Republic," American Journal of Tropical
Medicine and Hygiene, vol. 18, no. 6 (Nov. 1969),
1091-1210.

Hussey, E. R. J. "A Fiki's Clinic," Sudan Notes and Records, vol. 6 (1923).

Kendall, E. M. "A Short History of the Training of Mid-
wives in the Sudan," Sudan Notes and Records, vol. 33
(1952), 42-53.

Lambie, T. A. A Doctor Carries On. New York, 1942.

Osman, Abdel A'al Abdalla. "Milestones in the History of
Surgical Practice in the Sudan," Sudan Notes and Records, vol. 54 (1973), 139-152.

Squires, H. G. The Sudan Medical Service: An Experiment
in Social Medicine. London: Heinemann Medical Books,
1958.

Sudan Medical Journal. Journal published by the Sudan Medical Association, beginning publication in 1953.

ZOOLOGY AND WILD LIFE

Brocklehurst, H. C. Game Animals of the Sudan. Edinburgh: Gurney & Jackson, 1931.

Cave, F. O., and Macdonald, J. D. Birds of the Sudan.
Edinburgh: Oliver & Boyd, 1955.

Chapman, A. Savage Sudan, Its Wild Tribes, Big Game,
and Bird Life. Edinburgh: Gurney & Jackson, 1921.

Henriques, R. D. Q. Death by Moonlight: An Account of
a Darfur Journey. London: Collins, 1938.

Hurcomb, F. Angling in the Sudan. Khartoum: McCorquo-
dale, 1952.

Mackworth-Praed, C. W., and Grant, C. H. B. Birds of
Eastern and Northeastern Africa. London: Longmans,
1960.

Molloy, P. The Cry of the Fish Eagle: The Personal Experiences of a Game Warden and His Wife in the Southern
Sudan. London: Joseph, 1957.

Owen, T. R. H. Hunting Big Game with Gun and Camera.
London: Jenkins, 1960.

SOCIAL

ANTHROPOLOGY

Asad, Talal. The Kababish Arabs: Power, Authority, and
Consent in a Nomadic Tribe. New York: Praeger, 1970.

Barclay, Harold B. Buuri al Lamaab: A Suburban Village
in the Sudan. Ithaca, N. Y.: Cornell University Press,
1964.

_____. "The Nile Valley," in The Central Middle East, ed.
Louise E. Sweet. New Haven, Conn.: Human Relations
Area Files, 1968.

Baxter, P. T. W., and Butt, A. The Azande and Related

Peoples of the Anglo-Egyptian Sudan and Belgian Congo.
(Ethnographic Survey of Africa, edited by D. Forde,
Part 9.) London: International African Institute, 1954.

Bushra, El-Sayed, el-. "The Definition of a Town in the
Sudan," Sudan Notes and Records, vol. 54 (1973), 66-72.

_____. "Sudan's Triple Capital: Morphology and Functions,"
Ekistics, vol. 39 (April 1975), 246-250.

_____. "Towns in the Sudan in the Eighteenth and Early
Nineteenth Centuries," Sudan Notes and Records, vol. 52
(1971), 63-70.

Butt, A. The Nilotes of the Anglo-Egyptian Sudan and Uganda. (Ethnographic Survey of Africa, edited by D. Forde,
Part 4.) London: International African Institute, 1952.

Buxton, J. C. Chiefs and Strangers: A Study of Political
Assimilation Among the Mandari. Oxford, England:
Clarendon Press, 1963.

Cooper, M. C., and Schoedsack, E. B. "Two Fighting
Tribes of the Sudan (Messeria and Amarar)," National
Geographic Magazine, vol. 56 (1929).

Cunnison, Ian. Baggara Arabs. New York: Oxford University Press, 1966.

_____, and James, Wendy, eds. Essays in Sudan Ethno-
graphy Presented to Edward Evans-Pritchard. New York:
Humanities Press, 1972.

Deng, Francis Mading. Dinka Folktales: African Stories
from the Sudan. New York: Africana Publishing, 1974.

_____. The Dinka of the Sudan. New York: Holt, Rine-
hart & Winston, 1972.

_____. Tradition and Modernization: A Challenge for Law
Among the Dinka of the Sudan. New Haven, Conn.:
Yale University Press, 1971.

Evans-Pritchard, Edward Evan. The Azande, History and
Political Institutions. Oxford, England: Clarendon
Press, 1971.

_____. The Divine Kingship of Shilluk of the Nilotic Sudan
(Frazer Lecture 1948). Cambridge, England: Cambridge
University Press, 1948.

_____. Kinship and Marriage Among the Nuer. Oxford:
Clarendon Press, 1951.

_____. Man and Woman Among the Azande. London:
Faber & Faber, 1974.

_____. The Nuer. Oxford, England: Clarendon Press,
1940. Paperback Reprint in 1968.

_____. "The Nuer of the Southern Sudan," in African Po-
litical Systems, ed. M. Fortes and E. E. Evans-Pritchard. London: Oxford University Press, 1940.

_____. Nuer Religion. Oxford, England: Clarendon Press,
1940.

_____. The Political System of the Anuak of the Anglo-
Egyptian Sudan. (London School of Economics, Mono-
graphs on Social Anthropology, no. 4.) London: Lund,
Humphries, 1940.

_____. Witchcraft, Oracles, and Magic Among the Azande.
Oxford, England: Clarendon Press, 1937.

Gero, F. Death Among the Azande of the Sudan (Beliefs,
Rites and Cult). (Museum Combonianum, no. 22.)
Bologna: Editrice Nigrizia, 1968.

Hale, Sondra. Nubians: A Study in Ethnic Identity (African
and Asian Studies Seminar Series, no. 17). Khartoum:
Institute of African and Asian Studies, 1971.

Holý, Ladislav. Neighbors and Kinsmen: A Study of the
Berti People of Darfur. New York: St. Martin's Press,
1974.

Huffman, Ray. Nuer Customs and Folk-lore. London:
Cass, 1970.

Jackson, H. C. "The Khawalda Tribe," Sudan Notes and
Records, vol. 1 (1918).

Kennedy, J. "Mushuhara: A Nubian Concept of Supernatural

Danger and the Theory of Taboo," American Anthropologist, vol. 69 (1967), 685-702.

_____. "Nubian Zar Ceremonies as Psychotherapy," Hu-
man Organization, vol. 26 (1967), 185-94.

Kronenberg, A., and Kronenberg, W. "Parallel Cousins:
Marriage in Medieval and Modern Nubia," Kush, vol. 13
(1965), 241-260.

Lewis, B. A. The Murle, Red Chiefs and Black Commoners.
Oxford: Clarendon Press, 1972.

Lienhardt, G. Divinity & Experience, The Religion of the
Dinka. London: Oxford Press, 1961.

Luz, O. "Proud Primitives: The Nuba People," National
Geographic vol. 130, no. 5 (November 1966), 673-99.

MacGaffey, Wyatt. "History of Negro Migrations in the
Northern Sudan," Southwestern Journal of Anthropology,
vol. 17, no. 2 (1961), 178-97.

McLoughlin, Peter F. M. "Economic Development and the
Heritage of Slavery in the Sudan Republic," Africa
(Rome), vol. 33, no. 4 (Oct. 1962), 355-91.

_____. Language-Switching as an Index of Socialization in
the Republic of the Sudan. Berkeley: University of
California Press, 1964.

MacMichael, Harold A. The Tribes of Northern and Central
Kordofan. London: Cass, 1967 (reprint of 1912 ed.).

Mair, Lucy. Primitive Government. Harmondsworth, England: Penguin, 1962.

Myers, A. B. R. Life with the Hamran Arabs. London,
1876.

Nadel, S. F. The Nuba: An Anthropological Study of the
Hill Tribes of Kordofan. London, 1947.

Nicholls, W. The Shaikiya. Dublin: Hodges, Figgis & Co.,
1913.

Ogot, B. A. History of the Southern Luo. East African
Publishing House, 1967.

Owen, T. R. H. "The Hadendowa," Sudan Notes and Records, vol. 20 (1937), 183-208.

Paul, A. A History of the Beja Tribes of the Sudan. London: Cass, 1968 (reprint of 1954 ed.).

Queeny, E. M. "The Dinkas of the Sudan," Natural History
(New York), vol. 62 (1953), 84-90.

Sanders, G. E. R. "The Amarar," Sudan Notes and Records, vol. 18 (1935), 195-220.

_____. "The Bisharin," Sudan Notes and Records, vol. 16
(1933), 119-149.

Santandrea, Stefano. The Luo of the Bahr El Ghazal. Bologna: Editrice Nigrizia, 1968.

_____. A Tribal History of the Western Bahr El Ghazal.
Bologna: Editrice Nigrizia, 1964.

Seligman, C. G. "The Early History of the Anglo-Egyptian
Sudan," Scientific American, vol. 81 (1916).

_____. "The Hamitic Problem in the Sudan," Journal of
the Royal Anthropological Institute, vol. 42 (1913).

_____, and Seligman, B. Z. Pagan Tribes of the Nilotic
Sudan. London, 1932.

Singer, Andre, and Street, Brian V. Zande Themes.
Totowa, N. J. : Rowman & Littlefield, 1972.

Wall, L. L. "Anuak Politics, Ecology, and the Origins of
Shilluk Kingship," Ethnology, vol. 15 (April 1976),
151-162.

Westermann, E. The Shilluk People, Their Language and
Folklore. Philadelphia, 1912.

DEMOGRAPHY AND POPULATION

Balamoan, G. Ayoub. "Migration Policies and the Shaping
of the Sudanese Society," in Policy Sciences and Population, ed. W. F. Ilchman, et al. Lexington, Mass. :
Lexington Books /D. C. Heath, 1975.

_____. Migration Policies in the Anglo-Egyptian Sudan, 1884-1956. Cambridge, Mass.: Harvard University Center for Population Studies, 1976.

Barbour, K. "Population Shifts and Changes in the Sudan Since 1898," Middle East Studies, vol. 2, no. 2 (1966), 98-122.

Davies, H. R. J. "The West African in the Economic Geography of Sudan," Geography, vol. 49 (1964), 223-35.

Demeny, Paul. "The Demography of the Sudan, An Analysis of the 1955/56 Census," in The Demography of Tropical Africa, ed. W. Brass, et al, Princeton, N.J.: Princeton University Press, 1968.

Dzierzykray-Rogalski, Tadensz, and Prominska, Elizabeth. "The Influence of Ecological Factors Upon the Mortality Structure of the Inhabitants in the Wadi Halfa Region (Sudan)," African Bulletin, vol. 8 (1968), 41-56.

Henin, Roushdi. "The Level and Trend of Fertility in the Sudan," in Population Growth and Economic Development in Africa, ed. S. H. Ominde and C. N. Ejiogu. London: Heinemann, 1972.

_____. "Second Thoughts on Sudan's Population Census," in The Population of Tropical Africa, ed. J. C. Caldwell and C. Okonjo. New York: Columbia University Press, 1968.

Krotki, Karol J., ed. The Population in Sudan (Report on the Sixth Annual Conference). Khartoum: Philosophical Society of the Sudan, 1958.

_____. Travellers' and Administrators' Guesses of Population Size in XIX and XX Century, Sudan, Contrasted with Quasi-Stable Estimates. Edmonton: University of Alberta, 1975.

McLoughlin, Peter. "A Note on the Reliability of the Earliest Sudan Republic Population Estimates," Population Review, vol. 7 (1963), 53-64.

_____. "Population Growth Projections 1906-2006 for Economic Development in the Sudan," The American Journal of Economics and Sociology, vol. 24 (1965), 135-56.

Population Growth and Manpower in the Sudan. New York: United Nations, Department of Economic and Social Affairs, 1964.

Sudan. Ministry of Social Affairs. First Population Census of the Sudan, 1955-1956. Khartoum: Government Printing Press, 1958.

SOCIOLOGY AND SOCIAL CONDITIONS

Awad, M. "The Evolution of Landownership in the Sudan," Middle East Journal, vol. 25, no. 2 (1971), 212-28.

Coetzee, J. "Sudan's Ethnic Groups," Bulletin of the African Institute, vol. 9, no. 7 (August 1971), 291-5.

Fluehr-Lobban, Carolyn. "Women and Social Liberation: The Sudan Experience," in Three Studies on National Integration in the Arab World (Information Papers no. 12). North Dartmouth, Mass.: Arab-American University Graduates, 1974.

Haaland, Gunner. "Economic Determinants in Ethnic Processes," in Ethnic Groups and Boundaries, ed. H. B. Barth. Boston, Mass.: Little, Brown, 1969; pp. 58-73.

Hale, Sandra. "Nubians in the Urban Milieu: Great Khartoum," Sudan Notes and Records, vol. 54 (1973), 57-65.

Henin, R. "The Patterns and Causes of Fertility Differentials in the Sudan," Population Studies, vol. 23, no. 2 (1969), 171-98.

Lee, D. R. "Village Morphology and Growth in Northern Sudan," Proceedings of the Association of American Geographers (1969), pp. 80-84.

Lobban, R. "Alienation, Urbanisation and Social Networks in the Sudan," Journal of Modern African Studies, vol. 13, no. 3 (1975), 491-500.

McLoughlin, Peter F. M. "The Sudan's Three Towns: A Demographic and Economic Profile of an African Urban Complex," Economic Development and Cultural Change, vol. 12, nos. 1, 2, 3 (1964).

Nordenstam, Tore. Sudanese Ethics. Uppsala: Scandinavian Institute of African Studies, 1968.

Sudan. Department of Statistics. The Household Budget Survey in the Gezira-Managil Area. Khartoum, September 1965.

_____. Household Sample Survey in the Sudan, 1967-68, Pattern of Income and Expenditure. Khartoum, December 1970.

_____. Kadugli Household Budget Survey. Khartoum, September 1966.

_____. Omdurman Household Budget Survey. Khartoum, March 1965.

_____. Population and Housing Survey, 1964/66: Blue Nile Province Urban Areas. Khartoum, September 1968.

_____. Population and Housing Survey, 1964/66: Kassala Province Urban Areas. Khartoum, August 1968.

_____. Population and Housing Survey, 1964/66: Khartoum. Khartoum, Nov. 1965.

_____. Population and Housing Survey, 1964/66: Khartoum North. Khartoum, June 1966.

_____. Population and Housing Survey, 1964/66: Khartoum Province Urban Areas. Khartoum, September 1968.

_____. Population and Housing Survey, 1964/66: Kordofan Province Urban Areas. Khartoum, August 1968.

_____. Population and Housing Survey, 1964/66: Northern Province Urban Areas. Khartoum, July 1968.

_____. Population and Housing Survey, 1964/66: Omdurman. Khartoum, May 1966.

_____. Population and Housing Survey, 1964/66: Port Sudan. Khartoum, July 1966.

_____. Population and Housing Survey, 1964/66: Wad Medani. Khartoum, August 1966.

_____.____. Selected Tables from the 1970-71 Industrial
Survey. Khartoum, n. d.

Yassein, Osman.   "Social, Economic and Political Role of
Urban Agglomerations in the Developing States: The
Sudan's Experience," African Administrative Studies,
(Tangier), December 1967, pp. 1-11.

RELIGION

Allen, R. "Islam and Christianity in the Sudan," International Review of Missions, vol. 9 (1920).

Anderson, William B. Ambassadors by the Nile. London:
Lutterworth Press, 1963.

Barclay, Harold B. "Muslim 'Prophets' in the Modern Sudan," Muslim World, vol. 54, no. 4 (Oct. 1964), 250-255.

_____. "Muslim Religious Practice in a Village Suburb of
Khartoum," Muslim World, vol. 53, no. 3 (July 1963),
205-211.

_____. "A Sudanese Religious Brotherhood: al-tariqah al-
hindiya," Muslim World, vol. 53, no. 2 (April 1963),
127-137.

Cook, Christopher L. "The Church in the Southern Sudan,"
East and West Review (London), vol. 19, no. 4 (Oct.
1953), 119-125.

Daniel, Norman. "The Sudan," in Islam in Africa, James
Kritzeck and W. H. Lewis, eds. New York: Van
Nostrand-Reinhold, 1969; pp. 202-213.

Dempsey, J. Mission on the Nile. London: Burns and
Oates, 1955.

Evans-Pritchard, E. E. "Zande Theology," Sudan Notes and
Records, vol. 19 (1936).

Forsberg, Malcolm. Land Beyond the Nile. Chicago, Ill. :
Moody, 1967.

_____. Last Days on the Nile. Philadelphia, Penna. :
Lippincott, 1966.

Hasan, Yusuf Fadl. "The Penetration of Islam in the Eastern Sudan," in Islam in Tropical Africa, I. M. Lewis,
ed. London: Oxford University Press, 1966; pp. 144-159.

Hill, R. L. "Government and Christian Missions in the
Anglo-Egyptian Sudan," Middle East Studies, vol. 1,
no. 2 (1965), 113-134.

Hillelson, S. "The Anglo-Egyptian Sudan," in Islam Today,
A. J. Arberry and R. Landau, eds. London: Faber &
Faber, 1943; pp. 96-105.

_____. "Aspects of Muhammadanism in the Eastern Sudan,"
Journal of the Royal Asiatic Society of Great Britain
and Ireland, Part 4 (October 1937), pp. 557-577.

_____. "The People of Abu Jarid," Sudan Notes and Re-
cords, vol. 1, no. 3 (1918), 175-193.

Holt, Peter M. Holy Families and Islam in the Sudan.
Princeton, N. J.: Princeton University Program in Near
Eastern Studies, 1967 (reprinted in P. M. Holt, Studies
in the History of the Near East. London: Cass, 1973).

_____. "The Islamization of the Nilotic Sudan," in Northern
Africa: Islam and Modernization, M. Brett, ed. London: Cass, 1973; pp. 13-22.

Maan, W. J. "Church and State in the Sudan," Frontier
(London), vol. 7, no. 1 (1964), 36-40.

Nadel, S. F. "Two Nuba Religions: An Essay in Comparison," American Anthropologist, vol. 57, no. 4 (1955),
661-679.

Stevenson, R. C. "Some Aspects of the Spread of Islam in
the Nuba Mountains," in Islam in Tropical Africa, I.
M. Lewis, ed. London: Oxford University Press, 1966;
pp. 208-232.

Trimingham, J. S. The Christian Approach to Islam in the
Sudan. London: Oxford University Press, 1948.

_____. The Christian Church in Post War Sudan. London:
World Dominion Press, 1949.

_____. Islam in the Sudan. London: Cass, 1968 (reprint
of 1949 ed.).

Voll, John O. "Islam: Its Future in the Sudan," Muslim World, vol. 63, no. 4 (1973), 280-296.

_____. "Effects of Islamic Structures on Modern Islamic Expansion in the Eastern Sudan," International Journal of African Historical Studies, vol. 7 (1974), 85-98.

_____. "Mahdis, Walis, and New Men in the Sudan," in Sufis, Saints, and Scholars, N. Keddie, ed. Berkeley, Calif.: University of California Press, 1972; pp. 367-384.

Westermann, D. H. "Islam in the Eastern Sudan," International Review of Missions, vol. 2 (1913).

Willis, C. A. "Religious Confraternities of the Sudan," Sudan Notes and Records, vol. 4, no. 4 (1921), 175-194.

EDUCATION

Beshir, Mohamed Omer. Educational Development in the Sudan, 1898 to 1956. Oxford, England: Clarendon Press, 1969.

_____. "Some Problems of University Education in the Sudan," Comparative Education Review, vol. 5, no. 1 (June 1961), 50-53.

Bowman, H. Middle East Window. London: Longmans, 1942.

Burns, Donald. "Educational Development in the Sudan," Leeds African Studies Bulletin, (Leeds, England) vol. 6 (March 1967), 11-12.

Corbyn, E. N. "Bakht er Ruda: Institute of Education in the Sudan," Times Educational Supplement, December 1945, p. 604.

Currie, James. "The Educational Experiment in the Anglo-Egyptian Sudan, 1900-33," Journal of the Royal African Society, vol. 33, no. 133 (Oct. 1934), 351-71, and vol. 34, no. 134 (Jan. 1935), 41-60.

"A Functional Literacy Project in Sudan," UNESCO Chronicle, vol. 15, no. 2 (Feb. 1969), 70-71.

Gannon, E. J. "Education in the Sudan," Comparative Ed-

ucation Review, vol. 9, no. 3 (Oct. 1965), 323-50.

George, M. F. A. "Education for Self-government (A Discussion on Discipline in Sudanese Secondary Schools," Journal of Education, vol. 83 (1951), 328-30.

Griffiths, V. L. An Experiment in Education. London: Longmans, 1953.

_____. "An Experiment in Education in the Sudan," Overseas Quarterly, 1958, 49-51.

_____. "A Teacher Training and Research Centre in the Sudan," Overseas Education, vol. 16, no. 1 (Oct. 1944), 1-6.

Hodgkin, R. A. "The Sudan Publications Bureau," Overseas Education, vol. 19 (April 1948), 694-8.

Korbyn, E. N. "Kitchener School of Medicine," Journal of the Royal African Society, vol. 43 (1944), 66-68.

McIlroy, R. J. "Agriculture in the University of Khartoum," Nature, vol. 179 (1957).

Mynors, T. H. B. "A School of Administration in the Anglo-Egyptian Sudan," African Administration, vol. 2 (1950), 24-26.

Okeir, A. G. "Education Among the Beja," Overseas Education, vol. 23, no. 1 (Oct. 1951), 194-6.

Sanderson, L. "Education and Administrative Control in Colonial Sudan and Northern Nigeria," African Affairs, vol. 74 (Oct. 1975), 427-41.

_____. "Educational Development and Administrative Control in the Nuba Mountains Region of the Sudan," Journal of African History, vol. 4, no. 2 (1963), 233, 247.

_____. "Educational Development in the Southern Sudan, 1900-1948," Sudan Notes and Records, vol. 43 (1962).

_____. "Some Aspects of the Development of Girls' Education in the Sudan," Sudan Notes and Records, vol. 42 (1961).

_____. "Survey of Material Available for the Study of Ed-

ucational Development in the Modern Sudan, 1900-1963. "
Sudan Notes and Records, vol. 44 (1963), 69-81.

Scott, G. C. "Gordon Memorial College, Khartoum," African Affairs, vol. 48 (1949), 226-231.

Shepherd, G. "The National University in Multi-national
Societies: The Case of the Sudan," Africa Today,
vol. 14, no. 2 (1967), 9-11.

Tayeb, Salah el-Din el-Zein, el-. The Students' Movement
in the Sudan, 1940-1970. Khartoum: Khartoum University Press, 1971.

Tayyib, Griselda, al-. "Women's Education in Sudan," Kano
Studies (Kano, Nigeria), vol. 1 (Sept. 1965), 43-46.

Wingate, F. R. "The Story of the Gordon College and Its
Work," The Story of the Cape to Cairo Railway and
River Route 1887-1922, L. Weinthal, ed. London, 1923;
Part I, pp. 563-611.

HISTORY

EARLY HISTORY--ANTIQUITY TO A.D. 1500

Adams, William Y. "Continuity and Change in Nubian Cultural History," Sudan Notes and Records, vol. 48
(1967), 1-32.

_____. "Post-Pharoanic Nubia in the Light of Archeology,"
Journal of Egyptian Archeology, vol. 50 (1964), 102-120;
vol. 51 (1965), 160-178; vol. 52 (1966), 147-162.

_____. "Settlement Pattern in Microcosm: The Changing
Aspect of a Nubia Village During Twelve Centuries," in
Settlement Archeology, Kwangchih Chang, ed. Palo
Alto, Calif.: National Press Books, 1968.

_____. "The Seven Ages of Christian Nubia," Kush, vol. 12
(1964).

Arkell, A. J. "Early Khartoum," Antiquity, (1947), 172-181.

_____. Early Khartoum: An Account of the Excavation of

an Early Occupation Site Carried Out by the Sudan Government Antiquities Service in 1944-5.   London: Oxford University Press, 1949.

_____. A History of the Sudan from the Earliest Times to
1821. Westport, Conn.:   Greenwood Press, 1974 (reprint of the 2nd ed., 1961).

_____. The Old Stone Age in the Anglo-Egyptian Sudan.
Khartoum: Sudan Antiquities Service, 1949.

_____. Shaheinab, An Account of the Excavation of a Neo-
lithic Occupation Site Carried Out for the Sudan Antiquities Service in 1949-50.   London: Oxford University
Press, 1953.

Baikie, J.   Egyptian Antiquities in the Nile Valley.   London:
Metheun, 1932.

Balfour-Paul, H. G.   History and Antiquities of Darfur.
Khartoum: Sudan Antiquities Service, 1955.

Batrawi, A.   "The Racial History of Egypt and Nubia,"
Royal Anthropological Institute, vol. 75 (1945), and vol. 76
(1946), 131-156.

Budge, E. A. Wallis.   Annals of the Nubian Kings.   London:
Kegan Paul, Trench, Trubner, 1912.

_____. The Egyptian Sudan, Its History and Monuments.
Philadelphia, Penna.:   Lippincott, 1907.

_____. A History of Ethiopia, Nubia, and Abyssinia.   Lon-
don: Methuen, 1928.

Butzer, K. W., and Hansen, C. L.   Desert and River in
Nubia: Geomorphology and Prehistoric Environments at
the Aswan Reservoir.   Madison: University of Wisconsin Press, 1968.

Clark, J. Desmond.   The Prehistory of Africa.   New York:
Praeger, 1970.

Crawford, O. G. S.   Castles and Churches in the Middle
Nile Region.   Khartoum: Sudan Antiquities Service, 1953.

_____. "People Without a History," Antiquity, (1948), 8-12.

Crowfoot, J. W. The Island of Meroe. London, 1911.

Davidson, B. "The Mystery of Meroe: Remains of the Iron-using Kushite Civilization," History Today, (1958), 386-393.

Dunham, Dows. "Notes on the History of Kush, 850 B.C. -- 350 A.D.," American Journal of Archeology, vol. 50 (1946), 378-88.

_____. "Outline of the Ancient History of the Sudan, Part V: The Kingdom of Kush at Meroe and Napata," Sudan Notes and Records, vol. 28 (1947), 1-10.

Emery, Walter. Lost Land Emerging. New York: Scribner's, 1965.

_____. Nubian Treasure. London: Methuen, 1948.

"Excavations at Qasr Ibrim: New Light on the Still Enigmatic X-Group Peoples," Illustrated London News, 20 October 1962, pp. 605-607.

Fairservis, Walter A., Jr. The Ancient Kingdoms of the Nile. New York: New American Library, 1962.

Garstang, J.; Sayce, A. H.; and Griffith, F. L. Meroe-- The City of the Ethiopians. Oxford, England: Oxford University Press, 1911.

Greene, David Lee. Dentition of Meroitic, X-Group and Christian Populations from Wadi Halfa, Sudan. Salt Lake City, Utah: University of Utah Press, 1967.

Greener, L. High Dam Over Nubia. London: Cassell, 1962.

Hair, P. E. H. "Christianity in Medieval Nubia and the Sudan: A Bibliographical Note," Bulletin of the Society for African Church History, vol. 1, nos. 3-4 (1964), 67-73.

Hasan, Yusuf Fadl. The Arabs and the Sudan, from the Seventh to the Early Sixteenth Century. Edinburgh: Edinburgh University Press, 1969.

Haycock, B. G. "Mediaeval Nubia in the Perspective of Sudanese History," Sudan Notes and Records, vol. 53 (1972), 18-35.

_____. "Towards a Better Understanding of the Kingdom of Cush (Napata-Meroe)," Sudan Notes and Records, vol. 49 (1968), 1-16.

Hintze, Fritz, and Hintze, Ursala. Civilizations of the Old Sudan. Amsterdam: Gruner, 1968.

Irwin, H. T.; Wheat, Joe Ben; Irwin, Lee F. University of Colorado Investigations of Paleolithic and Epipaleolithic Sites in the Sudan, Africa. Salt Lake City, Utah: University of Utah Press, 1968.

Keating, Rex. Nubian Rescue. London: Hale, 1975.

_____. Nubian Twilight. London: Hart-Davis, 1962.

Kirwan, L. "The Decline and Fall of Meroe," Kush, vol. 8 (1960), 163-173.

_____. "Nubia and Nubian Origins," Geographic Journal, vol. 140, Part 1 (Feb. 1974), 43-51.

_____. "Nubia's Christian Age," UNESCO Courier, vol. 14 (1961), 38-39.

_____. "The X-Group Enigma," in Vanished Civilizations, E. Bacon, ed. New York: McGraw-Hill, 1963; pp. 55-78.

Leakey, L. S. B. "Review of the Old Stone Age in the Sudan," Man, vol. 52 (1952), no. 222.

Marks, Anthony; Scheneir, Joel; and Hays, T. R. "Survey and Excavations on the Dongola Reach (Sudan)," Current Anthropology, vol. 9, no. 4 (1968), 319-23.

Michalowski, Kazimierz. "Open Problems of Nubian Art in the Light of the Discoveries at Faras," in Kunst und Geschichte Nubiens in Christicher Zeit, E. Dinkler, ed. Recklinghausen: Aurel Bongers Verlag, 1970; pp. 11-28.

Mileham, G. S. Churches in Lower Nubia. Philadelphia, Penna.: University Museum, 1910.

Mukherjee, R., Rao, C., and Trevor, J. C. The Ancient Inhabitants of Jebel Moya, Sudan. London: Cambridge University Press, 1955.

Musad, M. M. "The Downfall of the Christian Nubian King-

doms," Sudan Notes and Records, vol. 40 (1959), 124-8.

Porter, B., and Moss, R. L. B. Topographical Bibliography of Ancient Egyptian Hieroglyphic Texts, Reliefs, and Paintings, 7. Nubia, the Deserts and Outside Egypt. Oxford, England: Clarendon Press, 1951.

Reisner, George A. The Archeological Survey of Nubia, Report for 1907-1908 (2 vols.). Cairo: National Printing Department, 1910.

_____. "The Meroitic Kingdom of Ethiopia: A Chronological Outline," Journal of Egyptian Archeology, vol. 9 (1923), 34-77, 157-60.

Sandford, K. S., and Arkell, W. J. Paleolithic Man and the Nile Valley in Nubia and Upper Egypt. Chicago, Ill. : University of Chicago Press, 1933.

Säve-Söderbergh, T. A. "The Nubian Kingdom of the Second Intermediate Period," Kush, vol. 4 (1956), 54-61.

Shinnie, Margaret. A Short History of the Sudan (Up to A. D. 1500). Khartoum: Sudan Antiquities Service, n. d.

Shinnie, P. L. "The Culture of Medieval Nubia and Its Impact on Africa," in Sudan in Africa, Y. F. Hasan, ed. Khartoum: Sudan Research Unit, 1971.

_____. Excavations at Soba. (Occasional Papers No. 3.) Khartoum: Sudan Antiquities Service, 1961.

_____. Medieval Nubia. Khartoum: Sudan Antiquities Service, 1954.

_____. Meroe, A Civilization of the Sudan. New York: Praeger, 1967.

_____. "New Light on Medieval Nubia," Journal of African History, vol. 6, no. 3 (1965), 263-73.

_____. "The Sudan," in The African Iron Age, P. L. Shinnie, ed. Oxford, England: Clarendon Press, 1971; pp. 89-107.

Trigger, Bruce. History and Settlement in Lower Nubia. New Haven, Conn. : Yale University Publications in Anthropology, 1965.

_____. "The Myth of Meroe and the African Iron Age,"
African Historical Studies, vol. 2, no. 1 (1969), 23-50.

_____. Nubia Under the Pharoahs. Boulder, Colo.: West-
view Press, 1976.

Vercoutter, J. "Sudanese Nubia and African History," United
Nations Review, vol. 8 (1961), 23.

Wendorf, Fred., ed. The Prehistory of Nubia. Dallas,
Texas: Southern Methodist University Press, 1968.

SUDANIC KINGDOMS, 1500-1800

Abu Selim, M. I. Some Land Certificates from the Fung
(Occasional Papers no. 2). Khartoum: Sudan Research
Unit, 1967.

Arkell, A. J. "Fung Origins," Sudan Notes and Records,
vol. 15, no. 2 (1932), 201-250.

_____. "History of Darfur, 1200-1700 A.D.," Sudan Notes
and Records, vol. 32 (1951), 37-70, 207-38, and vol. 33
(1952), 129-53, 244-75.

Bradford, J. S. P. "The Fung Kingdom of Sennar," Man,
vol. 52, no. 223 (1952).

Bruce, James. Travels to Discover the Source of the Nile,
1768-1773, 2nd ed. Edinburgh, 1805. 5 vols. A modern, abridged edition of this is Bruce of Kinnaird, Travels to the Sources of the Nile, ed. C. F. Beckingham.
Edinburgh: Edinburgh University Press, 1963.

Burckhardt, John L. Travels in Nubia. London: Gregg,
1968 (reprint of 1819 ed.).

Crawford, O. G. S. The Fung Kingdom of Sennar. Glou-
cester, England: Bellows, 1951.

Hillelson, S. "David Reubeni, An Early Visitor to Sennar,"
Sudan Notes and Records, vol. 16 (1933), 55-66.

_____. "The Fung Kingdom of Sennar (a letter)," Geograph-
ic Journal, (1952), 241.

_____. "Historical Poems and Traditions of the Shukria,"

Sudan Notes and Records, vol. 3 (1920), 33-75.

_____. "Tabaqat Wad DayfAllah," Sudan Notes and Records, vol. 6 (1923), 191-230.

Holt, Peter M. "Four Funj Land-charters," Sudan Notes and Records, vol. 50 (1969), 2-14.

_____. "Fundj," The Encyclopaedia of Islam, 2nd ed., II, 943-945.

_____. "Funj Origins: A Critique and New Evidence," Journal of African History, vol. 4 (1963), 39-55. (Reprinted in Studies in the History of the Near East.)

_____. "The Sons of Jabir and Their Kin," Bulletin of the School of Oriental and African Studies (London), vol. 30 (1967), 142-157. (Reprinted in Studies in the History of the Near East.)

_____. Studies in the History of the Near East. London: Cass, 1973

_____. "A Sudanese Historical Legend: The Funj Conquest of Soba," Bulletin of the School of Oriental and African Studies (London), vol. 23 (1960), 1-12.

Jackson, H. C. Tooth of Fire. Oxford, England, 1912.

Nalder, L. F. "Fung Origins," Sudan Notes and Records, vol. 14 (1931).

O'Fahey, R. S. "Kordofan in the Eighteenth Century," Sudan Notes and Records, vol. 54 (1973), 32-42.

_____. "Saints and Sultans: The Role of Muslim Holy Men in the Keira Sultanate of 'Dar Fur'," in Northern Africa: Islam and Modernization, M. Brett, ed. London: Cass, 1973; pp. 49-56.

_____. States and State Formation in the Eastern Sudan. Khartoum: Sudan Research Unit, 1970.

_____, and Spaulding, J. L. Kingdoms of the Sudan. (Studies in African History, no. 9.) London: Methuen, 1974.

Onwubuemeli, Emeka. "Early Zande History: The Origins

of the Avungara," Sudan Notes and Records, vol. 53
(1972), 36-66.

Paul, A. "Some Aspects of the Fung Sultanate," Sudan Notes
and Records, vol. 35 (1954), 17-31.

Robertson, J. W. "Fung Origins," Sudan Notes and Records,
vol. 17 (1934).

Robinson, A. E. "Abu el Kaylik, the Kingmaker of the Fung
of Sennar," American Anthropologist, n. s. vol. 31
(1929), 232-264.

_____. "The Regalia of the Fung Sultans of Sennar," Jour-
nal of the Royal African Society, vol. 30 (1930-1),
361-76.

Sadiq al-Nur. "Land Tenure in the Time of the Fung,"
Kush, vol. 4 (1956), 48-53.

Spaulding, J. L. "The Funj: A Reconsideration," Journal
of African History, vol. 13 (1972), 39-53.

"Tabaqat Wad Dayfallah." Kitāb al-Tabaqāt fī Khusūs al-
'Awliyā' wa al-Sālihin wa al-'Ulamā' wa al-Shu'arā',
Y. F. Hasan, ed.   Khartoum: Khartoum University
Press, 1971. (A partial translation of a different edi-
tion appears in vol. 2 of H. A. MacMichael, A History
of the Arabs in the Sudan.)

THE 19th CENTURY: TURCO-EGYPTIAN PERIOD

Ali, Abbas Ibrahim Muhammad. The British, the Slave
Trade and Slavery in the Sudan, 1820-1881. Khartoum:
Khartoum University Press, 1972.

Bethune, G. A Narrative of the Expedition to Dongola and
Sennar. Boston, Mass., 1823.

Brinton, Jasper Y. The American Effort in Egypt: A Chapter in Diplomatic History in the Nineteenth Century.
Alexandria, Egypt, 1972.

Crabites, Pierre. Gordon, The Sudan, and Slavery. New
York: Negro Universities Press, 1960 (reprint of 1933
ed.).

Gordon, Charles G.   Colonel Gordon in Central Africa,
1874-1879, George B. Hill, ed.   New York: Kraus,
1969 (reprint of 1885 ed.).

Gray, Richard.   A History of the Southern Sudan, 1839-89.
London: Oxford University Press, 1961.

_____. "Some Aspects of Islam in the Southern Sudan Dur-
ing the Turkiya," in Northern Africa: Islam and Modernization, M. Brett, ed.   London: Cass, 1973;
pp. 65-72.

Hajj, M. A., al-.   "The Nile Valley: Egypt and the Sudan
in the Nineteenth Century," in Africa in the Nineteenth
and Twentieth Centuries: A Handbook for Students and
Teachers, J. C. Anene and G. N. Brown, eds.   London: Nelson and Ibadan University Press, 1966;
pp. 163-180.

Hill, Richard L.   Egypt in the Sudan, 1820-1881.   London:
Oxford University Press, 1959.

_____. trans., ed., comp.   On the Frontiers of Islam:
Two Manuscripts Concerning the Sudan Under Turco-
Egyptian Rule, 1822-1845.   Oxford, England: Clarendon
Press, 1970.

_____, and Toniolo, Elias, eds.   The Opening of the Nile
Basin: Writings by Members of the Catholic Mission to
Central Africa on the Geography and Ethnography of the
Sudan, 1842-1881.   New York: Barnes & Noble, 1975.

Holt, Peter M.   "Modernization and Reaction in the Nineteenth Century Sudan," in P. M. Holt, Studies in the
History of the Near East.   London: Cass, 1973;
pp. 135-148.   (Originally appeared in William R. Polk
and R. L. Chambers, eds., Beginnings of Modernization
in the Middle East: The Nineteenth Century, Chicago,
Ill.: University of Chicago Press, 1968; pp. 401-415.)

Hoskins, G. A.   Travels in Ethiopia Above the Second Cataract of the Nile, Exhibiting the State of that Country
and Its Various Inhabitants under the Dominion of Mohammed Ali.   New York: Johnson Reprint, 1968 (reprint
of 1835 ed.).

Jackson, H. C.   Black Ivory and White: The Story of El

Zubeir Pasha Slaver and Sultan as Told by Himself.
New York: Negro Universities Press, 1970 (reprint of
1913 ed.).

Mercer, P. "Shilluk Trade and Politics from the Mid-
seventeenth Century to 1861," Journal of African History, vol. 12, no. 3 (1971).

Middleton, D. "The Search for the Nile Sources," Geographic Journal, vol. 138, no. 2 (June 1972), 209-224.

Nachtigal, Gustav.   Sahara and Sudan, IV. Wadai and Darfur,
trans. A. G. B. Fisher and H. J. Fisher. Berkeley,
Calif.: University of California Press, 1971.

Shukry, M. F.   The Khedive Ismail and Slavery in the Sudan
(1863-1879).   Cairo: Librairies La Renaissance d'Egypte,
1937.

White, Stanhope.   Lost Empire on the Nile: H. M. Stanley,
Emin Pasha and the Imperialists.   London: Hale, 1968.

MAHDIYYAH

Abu Salim, Muhammad I.   al-Murshid ilā Wathā'iq al-Mahdī.
(A Guide to the Documents of the Mahdi.) Khartoum:
Dār al-Wathā'iq al-Markaziyyah, 1969.

Alford, Henry S. L.   The Egyptian Soudan: Its Loss and
Recovery.   New York: Negro Universities Press, 1969
(reprint of 1898 ed.).

Ali, Abbas I. M.   "The British Military Officers and the
Sudan, 1886-1896," Sudan Notes and Records, vol. 54
(1973), 17-31.

_____.   "Contemporary British Views on the Khalifa's Rule,"
Sudan Notes and Records, vol. 51 (1970), 23-30.

Bedri, Babikr.   The Memoirs of Babikr Bedri, trans. Y.
Bedri and G. Scott.   London: Oxford University Press,
1969.

Bennett, Ernest N.   The Downfall of the Dervishes.   New
York: Negro Universities Press, 1969 (reprint of 1898
ed.).

Bermann, Richard A. The Mahdi of Allah, The Story of the
Dervish Mohammed Ahmed. New York: Macmillan, 1932.

Biobaku, Saburi, and al-Hajj, M. "The Sudanese Mahdiyya
and the Niger-Chad Region," in Islam in Tropical Africa,
I. M. Lewis, ed. London: Oxford University Press,
1966; pp. 425-44.

Brook-Shepherd, Gordon. Between Two Flags: The Life of
Baron Sir Rudolf von Slatin Pasha. London: Weidenfeld
and Nicholson, 1972.

Brown, L. Carl. "The Sudanese Mahdiya," in Protest and
Power in Black Africa, R. I. Rotberg and A. A. Mazrui,
eds. London: Oxford University Press, 1970. (Reprinted without notes in Rebellion in Black Africa, R. I.
Rotberg, ed., London: Oxford University Press, 1971;
pp. 3-23.)

Caillou, Paul. Khartoum. New York: New American Library, 1966.

Casati, G. Ten Years in Equatoria, trans. J. R. Clay.
London: Warne, 1891.

Charrier, Paul. Gordon of Khartoum. New York: Lancer,
1966.

Churchill, Winston L. S. The River War, 3rd ed. London:
New English Library, 1973.

_____. Young Winston's Wars: The Original Despatches of
Winston S. Churchill, War Correspondent, 1897-1900,
F. Woods, ed. London: L. Cooper, 1972.

Collins, Robert O. The Southern Sudan, 1883-1898, A
Struggle for Control. New Haven, Conn.: Yale University Press, 1962.

Cromer, Evelyn Baring, 1st Earl of. Modern Egypt. New
York: Macmillan, 1909. 2 vols.

Cuzzi, Guiseppe. Fifteen Years Prisoner of the False Prophet, Narrated by Guiseppe Cuzzi, comp. by Hans Reseher,
trans. by H. Sharma. Khartoum: Sudan Research Unit,
1968.

Daniel, Norman. Islam, Europe, and Empire. Edinburgh: Edinburgh University Press, 1966, chapter 15.

Dekmejian, R. , and Wyszomirski, M. "Charismatic Leadership in Islam: The Mahdi of the Sudan," Comparative Studies in Society and History, vol. 14, no. 2 (March 1972), 193-214.

Elton, Lord, ed. General Gordon's Khartoum Journal. New York: Vanguard, 1963.

Farwell, Byron. Prisoners of the Mahdi. New York: Harper's, 1967.

Fradin, Murray S. Jihad. New York, 1965.

Gessi Pasha, R. Seven Years in the Soudan. London: Gregg, 1967 (reprint of 1892 ed.).

Giffen, M. B. Fashoda: The Incident and Its Diplomatic Setting. Chicago, Ill. ; 1930.

Gordon, Charles George. The Journals of Major-General C. G. Gordon, C. B. at Khartoum. A. Egmont Hake, ed. New York: Negro Universities Press, 1969 (reprint of 1885 ed.).

Hill, Richard. Slatin Pasha. London: Oxford University Press, 1965.

Holt, Peter M. "The Archives of the Mahdia," Sudan Notes and Records, vol. 36 (1955), 1-10.

_____. The Mahdist State in the Sudan, 1881-1898, 2nd ed. Oxford, England: Clarendon Press, 1970.

_____. "Mahdiya in the Sudan, 1881-1898," History Today, vol. 8 (1958), 187-195.

_____. "The Place in History of the Sudanese Mahdia," Sudan Notes and Records, vol. 40 (1959), 107-112.

_____. "The Sudanese Mahdia and the Outside World, 1881-9," Bulletin of the School of Oriental and African Studies (London), vol. 21 (1958), 276-290.

_____. Three Mahdist Letter-books (1881-98)," Bulletin of

the School of Oriental and African Studies (London), vol. 18 (1956), 227-238.

Jackson, H. C.   Osman Digna.   London: Methuen, 1926.

Jackson, H. W.   "Fashoda, 1898," Sudan Notes and Records, vol. 3 (1920), 1-9.

Jephson, A. J. M.   Emin Pasha and the Rebellion at the Equator.   London: Sampson Low, et al., 1890.

Junker, Wilhelm.   Travels in Africa, 1875-1886 (3 vols.), trans. A. H. Keane.   London: Chapman and Hall, 1890-1892.

Marlowe, John.   Mission to Khartoum: The Apotheosis of General Gordon.   London: Gollancz, 1969.

Neufeld, Charles.   A Prisoner of the Khaleefa.   New York: G. P. Putnam's Sons, 1899.

Ohrwalder, Joseph.   Ten Years Captivity in the Mahdi's Camp, 1882-1892, trans. R. Wingate.   London: Sampson Low, Marston, 1892.

Power, Frank.   Letters from Khartoum.   London: Sampson Low, Marston, 1885.

Preston, Adrian, ed.   In Relief of Gordon: Lord Wolseley's Campaign Journal of the Khartoum Relief Expedition, 1884-1885.   London: Hutchinson, 1967.

Rehfisch, F., trans. and ed.   "Omdurman During the Mahdiya," Sudan Notes and Records, vol. 48 (1967), 33-61.

Sanderson, G. N.   "Conflict and Cooperation Between Ethiopia and the Mahdist State, 1884-98," Sudan Notes and Records, vol. 50 (1969), 15-40.

_____.   England, Europe, and the Upper Nile, 1882-1899. Chicago, Ill.:   Aldine Press, 1965.

Shaked, Haim.   The Life of the Sudanese Mahdi.   Edison, N. J.:   Transaction, 1976.

_____.   "A Manuscript Biography of the Sudanese Mahdi," Bulletin of the School of Oriental and African Studies

(London), vol. 32 (1969), 527-40.

_____. "The Presentation of the Sudanese Mahdi in a Unique
Arabic Manuscript," Tel Aviv: Tel Aviv University
Press, 1971.

Shibeika, Mekki. British Policy in the Sudan, 1882-1902.
London: Oxford University Press, 1952.

Slatin, Rudolf Carl von. Fire and Sword in the Sudan, trans.
F. R. Wingate. New York: Negro Universities Press,
1969 (reprint of 1898 ed.).

Stacey, Charles Perry. Records of the Nile Voyageurs,
1884-1885: The Canadian Voyageur Contingent in the
Gordon Relief Expedition. Toronto: Champlain Society,
1959.

Steevens, G. W. With Kitchener to Khartoum. New York:
Dodd, Mead, 1898.

Steffen, Don Carl. "Khartoum Tested British Empire,"
Smithsonian, vol. 4, no. 10 (Jan. 1974), 86-92.

Theobald, A. B. The Mahdiya: A History of the Anglo-
Egyptian Sudan 1881-1899. London: Longmans, Green,
1951.

Warner, Philip. Dervish: The Rise and Fall of an African
Kingdom. London: Macdonald, 1973.

Wingate, F. R. Mahdiism and the Egyptian Sudan, 2nd ed.
London: Cass, 1968 (reprint of 1891 ed.).

Wright, Patricia. Conflict on the Nile: The Fashoda Incident of 1898. London: Heinemann, 1972.

Wylde, Augustus. '83 to '87 in the Soudan. (2 vols.) New
York: Negro Universities Press, 1969 (reprint of 1888
ed.).

Ziegler, P. Omdurman. London: Collins, 1973.

ANGLO-EGYPTIAN SUDAN 1899-1956

Abbas, Mekki. The Sudan Question. London: Faber & Faber, 1952.

Abd al-Rahim, M. "Early Sudanese Nationalism, 1900-1938,"
    Sudan Notes and Records, vol. 47 (1966), 39-64.

_____. Imperialism and Nationalism in the Sudan: A Study
    in Constitutional and Political Development, 1899-1956.
    Oxford, England: Clarendon Press, 1969.

Artin Pasha, Yacoub. England in the Sudan, trans. G. Robb.
    London: Macmillan, 1911.

Atiyah, Edward. An Arab Tells His Story. London: Murray,
    1946.

Bakheit, Jaafar M. A. Communist Activities in the Middle
    East Between 1919-1927, with Special Reference to Egypt
    and the Sudan. Khartoum: University of Khartoum,
    1968.

Barawi, Rashed, el-. Egypt, Britain, and the Sudan. Cairo:
    Renaissance Bookshop, 1952.

Beshir, Mohamed Omer. Revolution and Nationalism in the
    Sudan. New York: Barnes & Noble, 1974.

Boustead, Hugh. The Wind of the Morning: The Autobiogra-
    phy of Hugh Boustead. London: Chatto and Windus,
    1971.

Collins, Robert O. "The Aliab Dinka Uprising and Its Sup-
    pression," Sudan Notes and Records, vol. 48 (1967),
    77-89.

_____. King Leopold, England, and the Upper Nile,
    1898-1918. New Haven, Conn.: Yale University Press,
    1968.

_____. Land Beyond the Rivers: The Southern Sudan,
    1898-1918. New Haven, Conn.: Yale University Press,
    1971.

Davies, Reginald. The Camel's Back. London: Murray,
    1957.

Duncan, J. S. R. The Sudan: A Record of Achievement.
    Edinburgh: Blackwood, 1952.

_____. The Sudan's Path to Independence. Edinburgh:
    Blackwood, 1957.

Henderson, K. D. D. The Making of the Modern Sudan:
The Life and Letters of Sir Douglas Newbold. Westport,
Conn.: Greenwood Press, 1974 (reprint of 1953 ed.).

_____. Survey of the Anglo-Egyptian Sudan, 1898-1944.
London: Longmans, Green, 1946.

Holt, Peter M. "Sudanese Nationalism and Self-Determination," in The Middle East in Transition, W. Z. Laqueur,
ed. New York: Praeger, 1958; pp. 166-186. (Appeared
originally in The Middle East Journal, vol. 10, 1956.

Hussey, E. R. J. Tropical Africa, 1908-1944. London:
St. Catherine Press, 1959.

Ibrahim, Hasan Ahmed. "The Policy of the Condominium
Government Towards the Mahdist Political Prisoners,
1898-1932," Sudan Notes and Records, vol. 55 (1974),
33-45.

_____. "The Sudan in the 1936 Anglo-Egyptian Treaty,"
Sudan Notes and Records, vol. 54 (1973), 1-16.

Jackson, H. C. Behind the Modern Sudan. London:
Macmillan, 1955.

_____. The Fighting Sudanese. London: Macmillan, 1954.

_____. Pastor on the Nile. London: SPCK, 1960.

_____. Sudan Days and Ways. London: Macmillan, 1954.

Keun, Odette. A Foreigner Looks at the British Sudan.
London: Faber & Faber, 1930.

MacMichael, H. A. The Anglo-Egyptian Sudan. London:
Faber & Faber, 1934.

_____. The Sudan. London: Benn, 1954.

Martin, Percy F. The Sudan in Evolution: A Study of the
Economic, Financial, and Administrative Conditions of
the Anglo-Egyptian Sudan. New York: Negro Universities Press, 1970 (reprint of 1921 ed.).

Nasr, Ahmed Abd al-Rahim. "British Policy Towards Islam in the Nuba Mountains, 1920-1940," Sudan Notes and
Records, vol. 52 (1971), 23-32.

Nigumi, M. A. A Great Trusteeship. London: Caravel, 1957.

Peel, Sidney. The Binding of the Nile and the New Soudan. New York: Negro Universities Press, 1969 (reprint of 1904 ed.).

Sanderson, G. N. "Sudanese Nationalism and the Independence of the Sudan," in Northern Africa: Islam and Modernization, M. Brett, ed. London: Cass, 1973; pp. 97-109.

The Sudan: A Record of Progress, 1898-1947. Khartoum: Sudan Government, 1947.

The Sudan: The Road Ahead (Report to the Fabian Colonial Bureau, Research Series no. 99). London: Fabian Publications, 1945.

Symes, S. Tour of Duty. London: Collins, 1946.

Theobald, A. B. Ali Dinar, Last Sultan of Darfur, 1898-1916. London: Longmans, 1965.

Voll, John O. "The British, the Ulama, and Popular Islam in the Early Anglo-Egyptian Sudan," International Journal of Middle East Studies, vol. 2 (1971), 212-218.

Voll, Sarah P. "The Introduction of Native Administration in the Anglo-Egyptian Sudan," Al-Abhath (Beirut), vol. 24 (1971), 111-123.

Warburg, Gabriel. "From Ansar to Umma: Sectarian Politics in the Sudan, 1914-1945," Asian and African Studies, vol. 9 (1973), 101-153.

_____. "Religious Policy in the Northern Sudan: Ulama and Sufism, 1899-1918," Asian and African Studies, vol. 7 (1971), 89-119.

_____. "The Sudan, Egypt, and Britain, 1899-1916," Middle East Studies, vol. 6 (1970), 163-178.

_____. The Sudan Under Wingate: Administration in the Anglo-Egyptian Sudan, 1899-1916. London: Cass, 1971.

Wingate, Ronald. Wingate of the Soudan, The Life and Time

of General Sir Reginald Wingate. Westport, Conn. :
Greenwood Press, 1975 (reprint of 1955 ed.).

INDEPENDENT SUDAN

Abdalla, I. "The Choice of Khashm al-Girba Area for the
    Resettlement of the Halfawis," Sudan Notes and Records,
    vol. 51 (1970), 56-75.

_____. "The 1959 Nile Waters Agreement in Sudanese-
    Egyptian Relations," Middle East Studies, vol. 7 (1971),
    329-342.

Bechtold, Peter. "Military Rule in the Sudan: The First
    Five Years of Ja'far Numayri," Middle East Journal,
    vol. 29 (1975), 16-32.

_____. Politics in the Sudan: Parliamentary and Military
    Rule in an Emerging African Nation. New York: Prae-
    ger, 1976.

Collins, C. "Colonialism and Class Struggle in Sudan,"
    MERIP Reports, no. 46 (April 1976), 3-17.

Corbe, K. "Sudan at the Crossroads," Review of Interna-
    tional Affairs, vol. 23, nos. 526-7 (5 March-20 March
    1972), 18ff.

Crawford, R. "Sudan: The Revolution of October, 1964,"
    Mawazo (Kampala), vol. 1, no. 2 (1967), 47-60.

Dafalla, Hassan. The Nubian Exodus. London: Hurst, 1975.

Grundy, K. "Nationalism and Separatism in East Africa,"
    Current History, vol. 54, no. 318 (February 1968), 90-4,
    112-3.

Gutteridge, W. F. Military Regimes in Africa. New York:
    Barnes & Noble, 1975.

Haddad, George M. Revolution and Military Rule in the
    Middle East. Volume 3. The Arab States: Egypt, the
    Sudan, Yemen, and Libya. New York: Speller, 1973.

Hasan, Y. F. "Sudanese Revolution of October 1964," Jour-
    nal of Modern African Studies, vol. 5, no. 4 (Jan. 1968),
    491-509.

Horton, Alan. "The Social Dimension of Sudanese Politics,"
    AUFS Reports Service, Northeast Africa Series, vol. 11,
    no. 4 (1964).

Kilner, P. "Better Outlook for Sudan," World Today, vol.
    28, no. 4 (April 1972), 181-8.

Kyle, K. "The Sudan Today," African Affairs, vol. 65,
    no. 260 (July 1966), 233-44.

Legum, C. "Sudan's Problems," Venture, vol. 23, no. 10
    (Nov. 1971), 16-20.

_____. "Sudan's Three-day Revolution," Africa Report,
    vol. 16, no. 7 (Oct. 1971), 12-15.

Niblock, T. "A New Political System in Sudan," African
    Affairs, vol. 73, no. 293 (Oct. 1974), 408-418.

Nyquist, T. E. "The Sudan: Prelude to Elections," Middle
    East Journal, vol. 19, no. 3 (Summer 1965), 263-272.

Said, Beshir Mohammed. The Sudan: Crossroads of Africa.
    London: Bodley Head, 1965.

Seidlitz, P. "Sudan: Breadbasket of the Arab World,"
    Swiss Review of World Affairs, vol. 25, no. 9 (Dec.
    1975), 12-16.

Sharma, B. "Elections in the Sudan During the Military
    Regime," Parliamentary Affairs, vol. 20, no. 3 (1967),
    274-280.

_____. "Failure of 'Local-government Democracy' in the
    Sudan," Political Studies, vol. 15, no. 1 (Feb. 1967),
    62-71.

_____. "The 1965 Elections in the Sudan," Political Quart-
    erly, vol. 37, no. 4 (1966), 441-452.

Shaw, D. "Resettlement from the Nile in Sudan," Middle
    East Journal, vol. 21, no. 4 (1967), 463-487.

Shibeika, Mekki. The Independent Sudan. New York:
    Speller, 1959.

"The Sudan Arbitration," Netherlands International Law Re-
    view, vol. 27, no. 2 (1970), 200-22.

POLITICAL

GOVERNMENT, ADMINISTRATION, POLITICS

Abbas, Makki. "Local Government in the Sudan," Public
    Administration, vol. 28 (1950), 55-58.

Abd al-Rahim, M. "Arabism, Africanism and Self-Identifi-
    cation in the Sudan," Journal of Modern African Studies,
    vol. 8, no. 2 (July 1970), 233-250.

Aguda, O. "Arabism and Pan-Arabism in Sudanese Politics,"
    Journal of Modern African Studies, vol. 11, no. 2 (1973),
    177-200.

Ahmad, Abd al-Ghaffar Muhammad. Shaykhs and Followers:
    Political Struggle in the Rufa'a al-Hoi Nazirate in the
    Sudan. Khartoum: Khartoum University Press, 1974.

Ahmed, Rafia Hassan. Critical Appraisal to the Role of the
    Public Service Commission in the Sudan, 1954-1969.
    Khartoum: Tamaddon Printing Press, 1974.

Branney, L. "Local Government in the Sudan," Journal of
    African Administration, vol. 1 (1949), 143-56.

Broadbent, P. B. "Sudanese Self-Government," International
    Affairs, (1954), 320-30.

Buchanan, L. M. "Local Government in the Sudan Since
    1947," Journal of African Administration, vol. 5 (1953),
    152-8.

Corbyn, E. N. "Democracy in the Sudan: The Sudan Ad-
    visory Council," Political Quarterly, (1945), 135-8.

Deng, Francis Mading. Dynamics of Identification: A Basis
    for National Integration in the Sudan. Khartoum: Khar-
    toum University Press, 1973.

Egyptian Society for International Law. Documents on the
    Sudan, 1899-1953. Cairo: 1953.

First, Ruth. Power in Africa: Political Power in Africa
    and the Coup d'Etat. Baltimore: Penguin, 1970.

Gandy, Christopher. "Sudan 1972: Pragmatism Replaces

Ideology," New Middle East (London), nos. 42-43 (Mar-April 1972), 14-16.

Gosnell, H. F. "The 1958 Elections in the Sudan," Middle East Journal, vol. 12 (1958), 409-417.

Howell, John, ed. Local Government and Politics in the Sudan. Khartoum: Khartoum University Press, 1974.

James, Eric. Perspectives in Public Administration in Sudan; Proceedings of the Fourth Round Table, March 10-19, 1962. Khartoum: Institute of Public Administration, 1963.

Kamal Hussein Ahmed. Management Improvement in the Gezira Scheme. (Occasional Papers no. 8). Khartoum: Institute of Public Administration, 1966.

Khalid, M. "Ethnic Integration in the Sudan," Review of International Affairs, vol. 24, no. 548 (5 Feb. 1973), 22-6.

Kheiri, Osman. Coordinated Planning in the Sudan and the Netherlands: A Comparative Survey (Occasional Papers no. 5). Khartoum: Institute of Public Administration, 1965.

Lavrencic, K. "Interview with President Jaafar Nemeiry," Africa (London), no. 21 (May 1973), 24-27.

Mahjub, Muhammad Ahmad. Democracy on Trial: Reflections on Arab and African Politics. London: Deutsch, 1974.

Mirghani Hammour. "Management Improvement in the Sudan," Sudan Journal of Administration and Development, vol. 7 (1971), 40-51.

Nimeiri, Sayed. Taxation and Economic Development: A Case Study of the Sudan. Khartoum: Khartoum University Press, 1975.

Perham, M. F. "Parliamentary Government in the Sudan," Colonial Review, (1949), 82-83.

_____. "The Sudan Emerges into Nationhood," Foreign Affairs, vol. 27 (1947), 665-77.

"President Decrees New Organization of Government," Al-
    Ayyam (Khartoum), 14 Oct. 1971. U.S. Department of
    Commerce, Office of Technical Services, Joint Publica-
    tions Research Service, Translations on the Near East
    (JPRS: 54, 847, Series No. 694, 4 Jan. 1972, pp. 103-
    118.)

Rivkin, Arnold, ed. Nations By Design. Garden City,
    N.Y.: Doubleday, 1968; pp. 119-178: "Development
    Institutions in Historical Perspective: The Sudan."

Robertson, James. "The Sudan in Transition," African Af-
    fairs, 1953, pp. 317-327.

_____. Transition in Africa. New York: Barnes & Noble,
    1974.

Rouleau, Eric. "Sudan's Communists: Routed by Arabism,"
    Le Monde (Weekly English Edition), no. 123, 28 August
    1971, pp. 11-13.

Salih, Galobawi M. "Civil Service in a Changing Society,"
    (Proceedings of the Seventh Roundtable Conference, Insti-
    tute of Public Administration, Khartoum). Printed as a
    special issue of Sudan Journal of Administration and De-
    velopment, vol. 3 (1967).

_____. Decentralization in the Sudan: Challenges and Re-
    sponse (Occasional Papers no. 3) Khartoum: Institute
    of Public Administration, 1964.

Sen, S., and Abbas, Makki. "The General Election in the
    Sudan," Parliamentary Affairs, (1954), 320-330.

Shaked, Haim; Souery, Esther; and Warburg, Gabriel. "The
    Communist Party in the Sudan, 1946-1971," in The USSR
    and the Middle East, M. Confino and S. Shamir, eds.
    New York: Wiley, 1973; pp. 335-374.

"Struggle in the Sudanese Communist Party," Al-Nahar
    (Beirut), 26-31 March and 1-3 April 1971. U.S. Depart-
    ment of Commerce, Office of Technical Services, Joint
    Publications Research Service, Translations on the Near
    East (JPRS: 53, 946, Series No. 647, 31 August 1971,
    all of the issue).

"Sudan for the Sudanese Is the Threshold of Self-Determin-

ation," World Today, vol. 11 (1955), 421-30.

Sylvester, A. "Muhammad Versus Lenin in Revolutionary Sudan," New Middle East (London), no. 34 (July 1971), 26-28.

Tayeb, Hassan Abbasher, el-. "The Role of the Administrator in Developing Countries: The Sudanese Case," Sudan Journal of Administration and Development, vol. 4 (1968), 59-78.

Yassein, M. O. The Melut Agricultural Scheme (Sudan): A Community Development Scheme in Developing Areas (Occasional Papers No. 12). Khartoum: Institute of Public Administration, 1967.

INTERNATIONAL RELATIONS AND THE SUDAN

Baddour, Abd el-Fattah Ibrahim el-Sayed. Sudanese-Egyptian Relations. The Hague: Hijhoff, 1960.

Barbour, K. M. "New Approach to Nile Waters Problem," International Affairs, vol. 33 (1957), 319-330.

Bechtold, Peter K. "New Attempts at Arab Cooperation: The Federation of Arab Republics, 1971-?," Middle East Journal, vol. 27, no 2 (Spring 1973), 152-72.

Crary, Douglas D. "Geography and Politics in the Nile Valley," Middle East Journal, vol. 3, no. 3 (July 1949), 260-276.

Fabunmi, L. The Sudan in Anglo-Egyptian Relations, A Case Study in Power Politics, 1800-1956. Westport, Conn. : Greenwood Press, 1973 (reprint of 1960 ed.).

Horton, Alan W. "The Splendid Isolation of the Sudan: An Arab-Speaking Country Holds Itself Aloof--Even from the Arab World," American Universities Field Staff Reports Service, Northeast Africa Series, XI (June 1964), 39-48.

Howell, J. , and Hamid, M. B. "Sudan and the Outside World, 1964-1968," African Affairs, vol. 68, no. 273 (Oct. 1969), 299-316.

Ismael, T. "Sudan's Foreign Policy Today," International

Journal, vol. 25, no. 3 (1970), 565-75.

_____. "United Arab Republic and the Sudan," Middle East Journal, vol. 23, no. 1 (Winter 1969), 14-28.

Kheir, A. "Chinese in the Sudan," Eastern Horizons, vol. 12, no. 3 (1973), 45-47.

Mohammed Awad, "Egypt, Great Britain, and the Sudan," Middle East Journal, vol. 1, no. 3 (July 1947), 281-91.

O'Rourke, Vernon A. The Juristic Status of Egypt and the Sudan. Westport, Conn.: Greenwood Press, 1973 (reprint of 1935 ed.).

Voll, John O. "Unity of the Nile Valley: Identity and Regional Integration," Journal of African Studies, vol. 3, no. 2 (Summer 1976), 205-228.

LAW

Anderson, J. N. D. Islamic Law in the Modern World. New York: New York University Press, 1959.

_____. "Recent Developments in Shari'a Law in the Sudan," Sudan Notes and Records, vol. 31, Part 1 (June 1950), 82-104.

Fawzi, Sa'd ed-Din. "The Status of Foreigners in the Newly Independent Sudan," Civilizations, vol. 7 (1957), 343-56.

Gorman, J. P. The Laws of the Sudan. Khartoum, 1941.

Gow, J. J. "Law and the Sudan," Sudan Notes and Records, vol. 33 (1952), 299-310.

Gretton, G. "The Law and the Constitution of the Sudan," World Today, vol. 24, no. 8 (August 1968), 314-23.

Howell, P. P. A Manual of Nuer Law, Being an Account of Customary Law, Its Evolution and Development in the Courts Established by the Sudan Government. London: Oxford University Press, 1954 (reprinted by Oxford University Press, 1970).

Laws of the Sudan: Prepared and Arranged by Sir Charles

Cummings. C. H. A. Bennett, ed. (as at 15 July 1955).
11 vols. Khartoum, 1956.

Mahdi, Saeed M. A., el-. A Guide to Land Settlement and
Registration. Khartoum: Khartoum University Press,
1971.

Mayal, R. C. "Recent Constitutional Developments in the
Sudan, International Affairs, vol. 28, no. 3 (July 1952),
310-321.

Mufti, M. A., el-. The Evolution of the Judicial System
in the Sudan. Khartoum: Tamadon Press, 1959.

Mustafa, Zaki. The Common Law in the Sudan, An Account
of the "Justice, Equity and Good Conscience" Provision.
Oxford: Clarendon Press, 1971.

_____. "The Treatment of Exemption Clauses by the Sudan
Courts," Journal of African Law, vol. 11, no. 2 (1967),
119-136, and vol. 12, no. 3 (1968), 146-172.

Thompson, Cliff F. "The Sources of Law in the New Nations
of Africa: A Case Study from Sudan," Africa and Law,
T. Hutchinson, ed. Madison: University of Wisconsin
Press, 1968; pp. 133-176.

SOUTHERN SUDAN CONFLICT AND RESOLUTION

Abdel Rahim, M. "The Development of British Policy in the
Southern Sudan, 1899-1947," Middle East Studies, vol. 2,
no. 3 (April 1966), 227-49.

Abu Eissa, F. "Revolution Relieved Sudan's Southern Problem," Middle East International, no. 3 (June 1971),
pp. 50-52.

Adam, P. "A Proposed Solution to the Arab Problem in the
Sudan," Midstream, vol. 17, no. 9 (Nov. 1971), 59-63.

Adams, M. "Settlement in the Southern Sudan," Middle East
International, no. 12 (April-May 1972), 2-3.

Albino, Oliver. The Sudan: A Southern Viewpoint. London:
Oxford University Press, 1970.

Ankrah, K. "Sudan: The Church and Peace," Africa, no. 9 (May 1972), 58-63.

Ayouty, Y., el-. "Settlement of the Southern Sudanese Problem: Its Significance and Implications for the Future," Issue, vol. 2, no. 1 (1972), 10-12.

Barton, N. "The Sudan: A Bid to Balance Between Arab, African Worlds," International Perspectives, vol. 3 (1973), 49-54.

Bell, J. Bowyer. "The Sudan's African Policy: Problems and Prospects," Africa Today, vol. 20, no. 3 (Summer 1973).

Beshir, Mohamed Omer. The Southern Sudan: Background to Conflict. London: Hurst, 1967.

_____. The Southern Sudan: From Conflict to Peace. London: Hurst, 1975.

Betts, Tristram. The Southern Sudan: The Ceasefire and After. London: Africa Publication Trust, 1974.

Collins, Robert O. The Southern Sudan in Historical Perspective. Tel Aviv: Shiloah Center, 1975.

_____, and Herzog, R. "Early British Administration in Southern Sudan," Journal of African History, vol. 2, no. 1 (1961), 119-35.

Dak, O. Southern Sudan: The Primacy of Socio-economic Development. Khartoum: Ministry for Southern Affairs, 1971.

Eprile, Cecil. "Sudan, The Long War," Conflict Studies, no. 21 (March 1972), 1-19.

_____. War and Peace in the Sudan, 1955-1972. London: Newton Abbot, David and Charles, 1974.

Fellows, L. "The Unknown War in the Sudan," New York Times Magazine, 22 Sept. 1968, pp. 25-27, 122-130.

Garang, Joseph. On Economics and Regional Autonomy. Khartoum: Ministry for Southern Affairs, 1971.

Bibliography 158

———. "The Southern Sudan," African Communist, no. 37 (1969), pp. 41-55.

Gray, R. "The Southern Sudan," Journal of Contemporary History, vol. 6, no. 1 (1971), 108-20.

Howell, J. "Politics in the Southern Sudan," African Affairs, vol. 72, no. 287 (April 1973), 163-78.

Jamal, A. "Southern Sudan Diary," Africa Report, vol. 17, no. 6 (June 1972), 18-20.

Kabara, J. "Sudanese Strife," Bulletin of the African Institute, vol. 9, no. 2 (June 1971), 261-4.

Kyle, K. "The Southern Problem in the Sudan," World Today, vol. 22, no. 12 (Dec. 1966), 512-20.

Ladouceur, P. "The Southern Sudan: A Forgotten War and a Forgotten Peace," International Journal, vol. 30, no. 3 (1975), 406-427.

Lobban, R. "National Integration and Disintegration: The Southern Sudan," in Three Studies on National Integration in the Arab World. (Information Papers, No. 12.) North Dartmouth, Mass.: Arab-American University Graduates, 1974.

McClintock, D. "The Southern Sudan Problem: Evolution of an Arab-African Confrontation," Middle East Journal, vol. 24, no. 4 (1970), 466-78.

Mekki, M., el-. "Peace in the Sudan," Arab World, vol. 18, nos. 5-6 (May-June 1972), 28-31.

Morrison, G. The Southern Sudan and Eritrea: Aspects of Wider African Problems. London: Minority Rights Group, 1971.

Musa, O. "Reconciliation, Rehabilitation, and Development Efforts in Southern Sudan," Middle East Journal, vol. 27, no. 1 (1973), 1-7.

Oduho, J., and Deng, William. The Problem of the Southern Sudan. London: Oxford University Press, 1963.

O'Fahey, R. S. The Southern Sudan: Symposium of Con-

flicts in the Middle African Region. London: International Institute of Strategic Studies, 1971.

Peace and Unity in the Sudan: An African Achievement. Khartoum: Ministry of Foreign Affairs, 1973.

Roden, D. "Peace Brings Sudan New Hope and Massive Problems," Africa Report, vol. 17, no. 6 (June 1972), 14-17.

Sarkesian, S. "The Southern Sudan: A Reassessment," African Studies Review, vol. 16, no. 1 (April 1973), 1-22.

Shaffer, N. M. "The Sudan: Arab-African Confrontation," Current History, vol. 50, no. 295 (March 1966), 142-146.

Shepherd, G. "National Integration and the Southern Sudan," Journal of Modern African Studies, vol. 4, no. 2 (Oct. 1966), 193-212.

Sylvester, A. "The Tragedy and Hope of Southern Sudan," Civilizations, vol. 22, no. 1 (1972), 79-89.

Tutu, T. "Black Power in the Sudan--New Divisions in Africa," New Middle East, no. 34 (July 1971), pp. 21-25.

Wai, Dunstan M., ed. The Southern Sudan, The Problem of National Integration. London: Cass, 1973.

ECONOMICS

AGRICULTURE

Basinski, J. J. "Some Problems of Agricultural Development in the Southern Provinces of the Sudan," Sudan Notes and Records, vol. 38 (1957), 21-46.

Bee, J. M. "Some Aspects of Sudan Agriculture," Great Britain and East, vol. 51 (1938), 222.

Bunting, A. H. "Agricultural Research at the Sudan Central Rainlands Station, 1952-56," Nature, vol. 178 (1956), 1103-4.

Catford, J. R. "The Introduction of Cotton as a Cash Crop in the Maridi Area of Equatoria," Sudan Notes and Records, vol. 34 (1953), 153-71.

Corbyn, E. N. "Soil Conservation in the A-E Sudan," Nature, vol. 155 (1945), 70-1.

Davies, H. R. J. "Irrigation Developments in the Sudan," Geography, vol. 43 (1958), 271-3.

Graham, Anne. "Man-Water Relations in the East Central Sudan," in Environment and Land Use in Africa, M. F. Thomas and G. W. Whittington, eds. London: Methuen, 1969; pp. 409-445.

Hadari, A. M., el-. "Some Socio-economic Aspects of Farming in the Nuba Mountains, Western Sudan," East African Journal of Rural Development, vol. 7, no. 1-2 (1974), 157-76.

Jedrej, M. C., and Stremmelaar, G. "Guneid Sugar Scheme: A Sociological Consideration of Some Aspects of Conflict Between Management and Tenants," Sudan Notes and Records, vol. 52 (1971), 71-78.

Jefferson, J. H. K. "Hafirs or Development by Surface Water Supplies in the Sudan," Tropical Agriculture (Trin.), vol. 31 (1954), 95-108.

Khider, M. "Cooperatives and Agricultural Development in the Sudan," Journal of Modern African Studies, vol. 6, no. 4 (Dec. 1969), 509-518.

Lee, D. "The Location of Land-Use Types: The Nile Valley in Northern Sudan," Economic Geography, vol. 46 (1970), 53-62.

Low, E. The Marketing of Groundnuts in the Sudan. Reading, England: Department of Agricultural Economics, University of Reading, 1967.

Mahgoub, Sayed Mirghani. "Land Policy and Settlement in Sudan," in Land Policy in the Near East, El Ghonemy and Mohammad Riad, eds. Rome: United Nations Food and Agriculture Organization, 1967; pp. 175-88.

Medani, A. I. "Elasticity of the Marketable Surplus of a Subsistence Crop at Various Stages of Development,"

Economic Development and Cultural Change, vol. 23
(1975), 241-9.

_____. Principles of Agricultural Extension and Its Pros-
pects in the Sudan. Khartoum, 1958.

Oliver, J. "Problems of the Arid Lands: The Example of
the Sudan," in Land Use and Resources: Studies in
Applied Geography. London: Alden and Mowbray, 1968;
pp. 219-39.

Osman, M. Shazali, and El Hag, H. E. "Irrigation Practices and Development in the Sudan," Sudan Notes and
Records, vol. 55 (1974), 96-110.

Roden, David. "Lowland Farms for a Mountain People,"
Geographical Magazine (London), December, 1969,
pp. 201-206.

Saab, R. "A Basic Programme for the Development of Sudanese Agriculture, Arab Economics, vol. 6, no. 68
(Sept. 1974), 24-5.

Saeed, Abdalla Babiker Mohamed. The Savanna Belt of the
Sudan: A Case Study. Khartoum: Ministry of Cooperation and Rural Development, 1971.

Shaw, D. J., ed. Agricultural Development in the Sudan.
Khartoum: Philosophical Society of the Sudan, 1966.

Simpson, I. G. "New Approaches to Irrigated Farming in
the Sudan: Organization and Management," Land Economics, vol. 46, no. 3 (Aug. 1970), 287-96.

Sorbo, Gunner. Economic Adaptations in Khashm el-Girba:
A Study of Settlement Problems in the Sudan. Khartoum:
Sudan Research Unit, 1971.

Thomson, J. R. "Farming by Fire--Burning the Grass in
the Central Sudan for the Sorghums and Sesame Crops,"
World Crops, 1950, pp. 396-7.

Thornton, D. S. Contrasting Policies in Irrigation Development. Reading, England: University of Reading, 1966.

_____. "Human and Social Aspects of Irrigation Develop-
ment," in Economics of Irrigation Development: A

Symposium. Reading, England: Department of Agricultural Economics, University of Reading, 1969; pp. 50-63.

_____, and Wynn, R. F. "An Economic Assessment of the Sudan's Khasm el Gibra Scheme," East African Journal of Rural Development, vol. 1, no. 2 (Jan. 19, 1970), 8-10.

Tothill, J. D., ed. Agriculture in the Sudan. London: Oxford University Press, 1948.

United Nations Development Program and Food and Agricultural Organization. Land and Water Resources Survey in the Jebel Marrah Area, the Sudan. (FAO/SF:48/SUD-17) Rome: UNDP/FAO, 1968.

Vajda, A. De. Land and Water Problems in the A-E Sudan," Soil Conservation (Washington), vol. 14 (1949), 207-10.

Warren, C. J. "Sudan's Agriculture Moves Ahead Despite the Country's Economic Setback," Foreign Agriculture (Washington), vol. 22 (1958), 13-14, 21.

AGRICULTURE--GEZIRA SCHEME

Allen, R. W. "The Gezira Irrigation Scheme, Sudan," Journal of the African Society, vol. 25 (1926).

Beer, C. W. "The Social and Administrative Effects of Large Scale Planned Agricultural Development," Journal of African Administration, vol. 5 (1953), 112-118.

_____. "Some Further Comments on the Gezira," Geographical Review, vol. 44 (1954), 595-6.

Bochkarev, Yu. "A Trip to the Gezira," New Times (Moscow), vol. 6 (1958), 23-25.

Culwick, G. M. "Social Change in the Gezira Scheme," Civilizations, vol. 5, no. 2 (1955), 173-82.

Ferguson, H. "The Gezira Scheme in the A-E Sudan," Agricultural Journal, (Jan.-Mar. 1952), 15-18, 50-56, 98-102.

_____. "The Gezira Scheme," World Crops, vol. 4 (1952).

Gaitskell, A. Gezira, A Story of Development in the Sudan.
London: Faber & Faber, 1959.

_____. "The Gezira Scheme of Social and Economic Development; History from 1898," Journal of the Royal Society of Arts, (1955), 67-86.

_____. "Planned Regional Development in Under-developed Countries: Reflections from Experience in the Gezira Scheme in the Sudan." From the background papers to the Duke of Edinburgh Conference, 1956. Volume 2 (1957), 77-88.

_____. "The Sudan Gezira Scheme for Irrigation," United Empire, (1952), 243-7, and Colonial Review, (1952), 235-7.

_____. "The Sudan Gezira Scheme for Irrigation and Its Economic and Political Significance," African Affairs, (1952), 306-13.

Gezira Scheme from Within. Khartoum: Sudan Gezira Board, 1954.

Hance, William A. African Economic Development, rev. ed. New York: Praeger, 1967.

_____. "The Gezira: An Example in Development," Geographical Review, vol. 44 (1954), 253-70.

_____. "The Gezira Scheme in the A-E Sudan: An Example in the Development of Less Developed Areas," Annals of the Association of American Geographers, vol. 43 (1953), 171.

Hassan, Farah, and Apaya, William Andrea. "Agricultural Credit in the Gezira," Sudan Notes and Records, vol. 54 (1973), 104-115.

Inge, E. "A Day in the Life of a Cotton Inspector in the Sudan," Empire Cotton Growing Review, April 1935.

Khalil, H. M. M. "The Sudan Gezira Scheme: Some Institutional and Administrative Aspects," Journal of Administration Overseas, vol. 9, no. 4 (Oct. 1970), 273-285.

King-Hall, M. Somehow Overdone: A Sudan Scrapbook.

London: Peter Davies, 1942.

Lambert, A. R. "The Sudan Gezira--The Land and the
    People," Geographical Magazine, vol. 9 (1939), 43-58,
    127-44.

Lan, H. L. "The Gezira Scheme; Results of an Irrigation
    Project in the Sudan," Tijds. econ. soc. G. (Rotter-
    dam), vol. 48 (1957), 183-7.

Langley, M. "Achievements of Sudan Cotton Plantations
    Syndicate," Crown Colonist, 1949, pp. 279-81.

Medani, A. I. "Consumption Patterns of the Gezira-Managil
    Tenants," Sudan Notes and Records, vol. 52 (1971), 79-87.

Melamid, A. "Egypt and the Gezira Irrigation Scheme of the
    Sudan," Middle East Affairs, vol. 4 (1953), 87-90.

Miller, R. "New Land for Africa: Irrigation in the Gezira,"
    Corona, vol. 3 (1951), 148-50.

Shaw, D. J. "The Managil South-Western Extension: An
    Extension of the Gezira Scheme," Tijdschrift van het
    Koninklijk Nederlandsch Aardrijkskundig Genootschap,
    82 (1965)-

_____, and Suleiman, A. A. "Stabilization Policies in De-
    veloping Countries: A Study Case of the Gezira Scheme,"
    Agricultural Economics Bulletin, UN, December 1965.

Simpson, S. R. "Land Tenure Aspects of the Gezira Scheme
    in the Sudan," Journal of African Administration, vol. 9
    (1957), 92-95.

Taha, T. "The Gezira Scheme Extensions--A Case Study,"
    Journal of Administration Overseas, vol. 14, no. 4
    (Oct. 1975), 240-250.

This Is Our Way to Build a Strong Nation: The Gezira
    Scheme. Khartoum: Ministry of Social Affairs, 1958.

Thornton, D. S. "Agricultural Development in the Gezira
    Scheme," Sudan Notes and Records, vol. 53 (1972),
    98-113.

Van der Kolff, G. H. The Social Aspects of the Gezira

Scheme in the Sudan. Amsterdam: Royal Tropical
Institute, 1957.

Versluys, J. N. D. "The Gezira Scheme in the Sudan and
the Ruman Kolhoz: A Comparison of Two Experiments,"
Economic Development and Cultural Change, vol. 2
(1953), 32-59.

Willis, C. A. "Gezira Cotton Scheme," Fortnightly, 1949,
pp. 330-336.

AGRICULTURE--ZANDE SCHEME

Ferguson, H. "The Zande Scheme," Empire Cotton Growers
Review, vol. 26, no. 2 (1949), 109-21.

_____, and McCall, A. G. "The Zande Scheme in the A-E
Sudan," World Crops, 1951, pp. 23-26.

Hance, W. A. "Zande Scheme in the A-E Sudan," Economic
Geography, vol. 31 (1955), 149-56.

Onwubuemeli, E. "Agriculture, the Theory of Economic
Development, and the Zande Scheme," Journal of Modern
African Studies, vol. 12 (1974), 569-87.

Reining, C. C. "The History of Policy in the Zande Scheme,"
The Proceedings of the Minnesota Academy of Science,
vol. 27 (1959), 6-13.

_____. "The Role of Money in the Zande Economy," Amer-
ican Anthropologist, vol. 64, no. 2, Part 1 (1962), 39-43.

_____. "The Zande Development Scheme," East African
Institute of Social Research, Report of the 2nd Joint
Conference, Feb. 1953, pp. 172-6.

_____. "Zande Markets and Commerce," in Markets in
Africa, P. J. Bohannan and G. Dalton, eds. Evanston,
Ill.: Northwestern University Press, 1963.

_____. The Zande Scheme: An Anthropological Case Study
of Economic Development in Africa. Evanston, Ill.:
Northwestern University Press, 1966.

Schlippe, P. de. Shifting Cultivation in Africa: The Zande

System of Agriculture. London: Routledge & Kegan Paul, 1956.

Willimott, S. G., and Anthony, K. R. M. "Agricultural Research and Development in the S. W. Sudan. Part 1. The Zande Scheme," Tropical Agriculture, vol. 34 (1957), 239-48.

Wright, J. W. The Zande Scheme from the Survey Point of View. Khartoum: Survey Department, Sudan Government, n. d.

Wyld, J. W. G. "The Zande Scheme," Sudan Notes and Records, vol. 30 (1949), 37-57.

DEVELOPMENT, FINANCE, ADMINISTRATION

Agraa, A., el-. "The Sudan and the Arab Customs Union: A Conflict," East African Economic Review, vol. 1, no. 2 (1969), 39-51.

Ahmed, Hassan A/Aziz. "Aspects of Sudan's Foreign Trade During the 19th Century," Sudan Notes and Records, vol. 55 (1974), 16-32.

Ali, Ali Abdalla, "The Sudan's Invisible Trade, 1956-1969: A Brief Survey," Sudan Notes and Records, vol. 54 (1973), 124-38.

Ali, Ali Abdel Hamid. Measures for Stimulating the Private Sector in Sudanese Economic Development. Khartoum: Institute of Public Administration, 1968.

Ali, Mohamed Abdel Rahman. "Calculating the Contribution of a Structural Shift to Economic Growth in the Sudan, 1955-1967," Sudan Notes and Records, vol. 54 (1973), 116-123.

_____. Fluctuations and Impact of Government Expenditure in the Sudan, 1955-1967. Khartoum: Khartoum University Press, 1974.

_____. Government Expenditure and Economic Development, A Case Study of the Sudan. Khartoum: Khartoum University Press, 1974.

_____. "The Propensity to Consume and Economic Develop-
ment in a Dual Economy: Sudan, 1955-1967," Sudan
Notes and Records, vol. 53 (1972), 114-122.

_____, and Kamal Abdel Gadir Salim. "Export Taxes and
Fiscal Policy in Developing Countries with Special Reference to the Sudan," Sudan Notes and Records, vol. 55
(1974), 111-122.

Awad, Mohamed. "Government Policy Towards Private
Industry in the Sudan," L'Egypte Contemp., vol. 61,
no. 340 (April 1970), 61-80.

_____. "The Southern Sudan: Planning for National Inte-
gration," Sudan Notes and Records, vol. 55 (1974), 88-95.

Baloula, Ali Eid. Some Problems and Defects in Administration of Public Development Schemes in the Sudan.
Khartoum: Institute of Public Administration, 1969.

Bardeleben, Manfred. The Cooperative System in the Sudan.
Munich: Weltform-Verlag, 1973.

Blackenburg, Peter, and Klemens, Hubert. The Khashm el-
Girba Settlement Scheme in Sudan: An Appraisal for the
World Food Program. Berlin: Institut für Ausländische
Wirtshaft der Technischen Universität, 1969.

Bushra, F., el-. "Population Growth and Economic Development in the Sudan," Bulletin of Arab Res. and Studies,
no. 5 (June 1974), 3-11.

"Development of the Anglo-Egyptian Sudan," United States
Commercial Report, no. 240. Washington, 1913.

Fahim, Hussein M. Nubian Resettlement in the Sudan.
Miami, Fla.: Field Research Projects, 1972.

Goldberg, S. "Economic Position of the Anglo-Egyptian Sudan," Commerce Reports no. 34. Washington: U.S.
Bureau of Foreign and Domestic Commerce, 1940.

Güsten, Rolf. Problems of Economic Growth and Planning:
The Sudan Example: Some Aspects and Implications of
the Current Ten-Year Plan. Berlin: Springer-Verlag,
1966.

Hewins, H. P. "Economic Development in the Anglo-Egyptian Sudan," 3rd International Congress of Tropical Agriculture, 2 (1914).

Imam, Faisal B., ed. Industry in the Sudan, Papers Presented to the First Erkowit Conference, Sept., 1966. Khartoum: Government Printing Press, 1973.

Jack, Ahmed H., el-. The Sudan Management Development and Productivity Centre, An Evaluation of the First Phase of Operation, 1965-70. Khartoum: Khartoum University Press, 1973.

Kubinski, Z. M. Public Finance for Stability and Growth in an Underdeveloped Export Economy: A Case Study of the Republic of the Sudan. Amsterdam: International Bureau of Fiscal Documentation, 1961.

"Lights on Four Selected Development Plans," Arab Economist, no. 50 (March 1973), 6-9.

Mahdouk, A., and Drees, F. "Domestic Policies and Payment Problems of the Sudan, 1947-1962," International Monetary Fund Staff Papers, March, 1964.

Meagher, Robert F. Public International Development Financing in Sudan. (Public International Development Financing Research Project, Columbia University School of Law, Report No. 11.) New York: Columbia University, 1965.

Nimeiri, Sayed M. "Tax Incentives for the Promotion of Private Industry in the Sudan," Sudan Notes and Records, vol. 55 (1974), 123-33.

Osman, Omar, and Suleiman, A. A. "The Economy of Sudan," in The Economies of Africa, P. Robson and D. A. Lury, eds. Evanston, Ill.: Northwestern University Press, 1969, 436-70.

Philosophical Society of the Sudan, Modern Nation Building. Khartoum, 1971.

Sa'd al-Din Fawzi. Aspects of the Sudan Economy. Cairo: Arab League, Institute of Studies, 1958.

_____. "Problems of Economic Development in the Sudan,"

Presence Africaine (Paris), 1956, 28-45.

_____. "The Structure and Development of the Sudan Economy," Proceedings of the UNESCO Conference of Economic Development, Beirut, 1957.

Saeed, Osman Hassan. The Industrial Bank of Sudan, 1962-1968, An Experiment in Development Banking. Khartoum: Khartoum University Press, 1971.

_____. "Marketability of Securities as an Incentive for Voluntary Savings: A Case Study of the Sudan," Sudan Notes and Records, vol. 52 (1971), 88-100.

Sammani, M., al-. "A Study of Central Villages as Planning Units for the Sudan," Ekistics, vol. 32, no. 189 (August 1971), 124-33.

Shaw, D. J. "A Note on the Sudan's Ten Year Plan of Economic and Social Development," Agricultural Economics Bulletin for Africa, no. 3 (June 1963).

Stone, John. Sudan Economic Development, 1899-1913. Khartoum: Sudan Economic Institute, 1955.

_____. The Sudan Economy, Introductory Notes. Khartoum: Sudan Economic Institute, 1953.

Sudan. Economic Planning Secretariat. The Ten Year Plan of Economic and Social Development, 1961/62-1970/71. Khartoum: Government Printing Press, 1962.

_____. Ministry of Planning. The Five Year Plan of Economic and Social Development of the Democratic Republic of the Sudan for the Period 1970/71-1974/75. Khartoum, 1970.

Suleiman, Ali Ahmad. "Stabilization Policies for Cotton in the Sudan," in African Primary Producers and International Trade, I. G. Stewart and H. W. Ord, eds. Edinburgh: University Press, 1965.

Taha, El Waleed Mohamed. "From Dependent Currency to Central Banking in the Sudan," Sudan Notes and Records, vol. 51 (1970), 95-105.

United Nations. Structure and Growth of Selected African Economies. New York, 1958, Chapter 4, pp. 148-201.

Uthman, Umar Muhammad. "Social and Economic Development of the Sudan," International Labour Review, vol. 78 (1958), 329-47.

Verrier, Anthony. "Sudan: A Rethink Over Economic Policy," Middle East International (London), no. 4 (July 1971), 37-38.

Vries, Egbert de. Essays on the Economic Development of Africa. The Hague: Mouton, 1968, pp. 36-53.

Wahab, A. A. "The Financing of Economic Development in the Sudan--The Public Sector," Proceedings, Institute of Public Administration of the Sudan. Khartoum, 1962.

Wells, F. A. "Economic Development in the Sudan," The Three Banks Review, no. 61 (March 1964).

Wilmington, M. W. "Aspects of Moneylending (shayl) in Northern Sudan," Middle East Journal, vol. 9 (1955), 139-46.

Wynn, R. "The Sudan's 10-Year Plan of Economic Development 1961/62-1970/71: An Analysis of Achievement to 1967-68," Journal of Developing Areas, vol. 5, no. 4 (July 1971) 555-76.

Yacoub, el Sammani A., and Agabani, Fouad A. Scientific and Technical Potential "STP" in the Sudan. Khartoum: Khartoum University Press, 1974.

LABOR

Kitchen, Helen. "Trade Unions: Communist Stronghold," Africa Special Report, vol. 4, no. 1 (January 1959), 12 and 16.

McLoughlin, P. F. M. "Labour Market Conditions and Wages in the Three Towns, 1900-1950," Sudan Notes and Records, vol. 51 (1970), 105-118.

Milne, Janet C. M. "The Impact of Labour Migration on the Umarar in Port Sudan," Sudan Notes and Records, vol. 55 (1974), 70-87.

Sa'd al-Din Fawzi. "Joint Consultation in Sudan Industry:

A Critical Analysis of the Attempt to Form Works Committee in the Sudan," Sudan Notes and Records, vol. 35 (1954), 32-49.

_____. "Labour Force of Sudan," in The Population of the Sudan, Report on the Sixth Annual Conference of the Philosophical Society of the Sudan. Khartoum, 1958.

_____. The Labour Movement in the Sudan, 1946-1955. London: Oxford University Press, 1957.

_____. "The Wage Structure and Wage Policy in the Sudan," Sudan Notes and Records, vol. 36 (1955), 159-75.

Taha, Abdel Rahman E. Ali. "Reflections on the Structure and Government of the Sudan Railway Workers' Union," Sudan Notes and Records, vol. 55 (1974), 61-69.

_____, and el Jack, Ahmed H. The Regulation of Termination of Employment in the Sudanese Private Sector. Khartoum: Khartoum University Press, 1973.

APPENDICES

FUNJ SULTANS OF SANNAR

1. Amara Dunkas (1504-1534)
2. Nayil ibn Amara (1534-1551)
3. Abd al-Qadir I ibn Amara (1551-1558)
4. Amara II Abu Sakikin ibn Nayil (1558-1569)
5. Dakin al-'Adil ibn Nayil (1569-1586)
6. Dawra ibn Dakin (1586-1587)
7. Tabl ibn Abd al-Qadir I (1587-1591)
8. Unsa I, ibn Tabl (1592-1604)
9. Abd al-Qadir II, ibn Unsa I (1604-1606)
10. Adlan I, ibn Unsa I (1606-1611)
11. Badi I, ibn Abd al-Qadir II, Sayyid al-Qawm (1611-1617)
12. Rubat I, ibn Badi I (1617-1645)
13. Badi II Abu Diqn ibn Rubat I (1645-1681)
14. Unsa II, ibn Nasir ibn Rubat (1681-1692)
15. Badi III al-Ahmar ibn Unsa II (1692-1716)
16. Unsa III ibn Badi III (1716-1720)
17. Nul [not of the old royal line] (1720-1724)
18. Badi IV Abu Shulukh ibn Nul (1724-1762)

Sultans of the Hamaj regency:

19. Nasir ibn Badi IV (1762-1769)
20. Ismail ibn Badi IV (1769-1776)
21. Adlan II, ibn Ismail (1776-1789)
22. Awkal (1789)
23. Tabl (1789)
24. Badi V, Ibn Tabl (1790)
25. Hasab Rabbihi (1790)
26. Nawwar (1790-1791)
27. Badi VI, ibn Tabl (1791-1821)

KEIRA SULTANS OF DARFUR
(dates of accession, or estimates, given where known)

1. Sulayman Solong (ca. 1640)
2. Musa ibn Sulayman
3. Ahmad Bakr ibn Musa
4. Muhammad Dawra ibn Ahmad Bakr
5. Umar ibn Muhammad Dawra (ca. 1743)
6. Abu al-Qasim ibn Ahmad Bakr (ca. 1749)
7. Muhammad Tayrab ibn Ahmad Bakr (ca. 1756)
8. Abd al-Rahman al-Rashid ibn Ahmad Bakr (ca. 1787)
9. Muhammad al-Fadl ibn Abd al-Rahman (1801)
10. Muhammad Husayn ibn Muhammad Fadl (1839)
11. Ibrahim ibn Muhammad Husayn (1873)

Pretenders to the throne during the period of Turco-Egyptian and Mahdist rule in Darfur (1874-1898):

12. Hasab Allah ibn Muhammad Fadl
13. Bush ibn Muhammad Fadl
14. Harun ibn Sayf al-Din ibn Muhammad Fadl
15. Abdallah Dud Banja ibn Bakr ibn Muhammad Fadl
16. Yusuf ibn Ibrahim
17. Abu al-Khayrat ibn Ibrahim

The revived sultanate:

18. Ali Dinar ibn Zakariyya ibn Muhammad Fadl (1898)

TURCO-EGYPTIAN GOVERNORS IN THE 19th CENTURY
(list based on Na'um Shuqayr, Ta'rikh al-Sudan, III)

1. Uthman Bey (1825-1826)
2. Mahhu Bey (1826)
3. Khurshid Pasha (1826-1839)
4. Ahmad Pasha Abu Wadan (1839-1844)
5. Ahmad Pasha al-Manikli (1844-1845)
6. Khalid Pasha (1846-1850)
7. Abd al-Latif Pasha (1850-1851)
8. Rustum Pasha (1851-1852)
9. Ismail Pasha Abu Jabal (1852-1853)
10. Salim Pasha (1853-1854)
11. Ali Pasha Sirri (1854-1855)
12. Ali Pasha Jarkis (1855-1857)
13. Arakil Bey al-Armani (1857-1859)
14. Hasan Bey Salamah (1859-1862)
15. Muhammad Bey Rasikh (1862-1863)
16. Musa Pasha Hamdi (1863-1865)
17. Ja'far Pasha Sadiq (1865)
18. Ja'far Pasha Mazhar (1866-1871)

19. Mumtaz Pasha (1871-1873)
20. Ismail Pasha Ayyub (1873-1877)
21. Gordon Pasha (1877-1879)
22. Ra'uf Pasha (1879-1882)
23. Abd al-Qadir Pasha Hilmi (1882-1883)
24. 'Ala al-Din Pasha Siddiq (1883)
25. Gordon Pasha (second time; 1884-1885)

20th-CENTURY GOVERNMENT LEADERS

Governors-General of the Anglo-Egyptian Sudan:

1898-1899 H. H. Kitchener
1899-1916 F. Reginald Wingate
1916-1924 Lee Stack
1924-1926 Geoffrey Archer
1926-1934 John Maffey
1934-1940 Stewart Symes
1940-1947 Hubert Huddleston
1947-1955 Robert Howe
1955   Knox Helm

Heads of Government of the Independent Sudan:

1954-1956 Ismail al-Azhari (prime minister, including era
          of "self-government")
1956-1958 Abdallah Khalil (prime minister)
1958-1964 Ibrahim Abboud (president and head of the Supreme
          Military Council)
1964-1965 Sirr al-Khatim al-Khalifah (prime minister)
1965-1966 Muhammad Ahmad Mahjub (prime minister)
1966-1967 Sadiq al-Mahdi (prime minister)
1967-1969 Muhammad Ahmad Mahjub (prime minister)
1969   Babikr Awadallah (prime minister)
1969-   Ja'far al-Numayri (prime minister and president)